なぜ、
日本人は？

Hard-to-Answer Questions about Japan

装丁 ——————————— スタジオ・ギブ（川島　進）
装画 ——————————— 小森哲郎
イラストレーション ———— 野崎一人
翻訳 ——————————— Michael Brase

Published by Japan Book Inc.
3-24-502 Kanda-Ogawamachi, Chiyoda-ku, Tokyo 101-0052

First Edition 2007

EJ
対訳
ブックス

なぜ、日本人は?

答えに詰まる外国人の質問178

Hard-to-Answer Questions about Japan

Uchiike Hisataka
内池久貴
＋Office Miyako［著］
Michael Brase
マイケル・ブレーズ［訳］

JapanBook

前書

「日本人はなぜ結婚式を神道でやって、葬式を仏教でやるの？」
——はじめてアメリカに行ったとき、日本に何度か来たことがある人から、こんな質問をされたときの驚きが忘れられません。

神様と仏様の両方を信じているということが、一神教の彼らにとっては驚きなのでしょうが、そんな疑問があるのだと知ったことが、私にとっては驚きでした。文化が違えば、そのはざ間に疑問が出てくるし、そういう疑問をぶつけられて初めて、自分の国の特殊性に気が付きます。

この本は、多くの本の執筆者であり編集者でもある内池久貴さんや、企画グループ Office Miyako の皆さんと語らい、こんな疑問を列挙したうえで、その回答を書いていただいたものです。

翻訳はマイケル・ブレーズさんにお願いしました。編集者として、翻訳者として日本経験が長いブレーズさんは、私たちの説明の足りないところを補うような丁寧な翻訳をしてくれました。また日本語に引きずられることのないネイティブな英語になっています。

このため、日本文と英文が対応していないところもありますが、むりやり合わせようとすると、説明がくどくなったり、おかしな文章になってしまいます。外国の人に話すときには、こんな説明まで入れたほうがいいのだということが分かり、また英語と日本語の違いも分かるので、このギャップはそのまま残すことにしました。

この本が、海外の人との交流に役立ってくれれば、こんな幸せなことはありません。

ジャパンブック代表
大村数一

Preface

"Why do Japanese have Shintō weddings but Buddhist funerals?" On my first visit to the United States, I was asked this question by an American who had been to Japan a number of times. I was so surprised by the question that I don't think I will ever forget it.

For someone who thinks that there is only one true religion, it is probably hard to believe that other people can believe in two—in this case, Shintō and Buddhism. If the questioner found this fact hard to believe, I found it equally hard to believe that such a question had even occurred to him. Until then, I had never given the matter a thought. When two cultures come together, questions of this kind arise, and for the first time you realize what is unique about your own culture.

The questions that appear in this book are the result of discussions with the staff of the editorial group Office Miyako and the editor and prolific writer Hisataka Uchiike, who provided the answers.

The translation was done by Michael Brase, editor, translator, and longtime resident of Japan. He has added bits of information that might be of use when talking to a foreigner, and has produced a natural-sounding text that almost makes you forget that you are reading a translation.

One side effect of this, however, is that there are times when the Japanese and English don't perfectly match. If we insisted that they match perfectly, no matter what, one or the other would end up sounding odd. As the translation stands now, you can learn what kind of extra information is needed and how a subject should be approached when talking with foreign friends or acquaintances. At the same time, you can appreciate the differences between the two languages. For these reasons, it was decided to leave the gaps between the original Japanese and the English translation as they are.

In conclusion, it would make me quite happy if this book proves to be of some help to readers in communicating with English-speaking people about Japanese culture.

Ohmura Kazuichi (Publisher, Japan Book Inc.)

目次

Contents

1 世界の中のニッポン

Qなぜ、最近、「ジャパン・クール」という言葉が人気なのですか？

クールという言葉は、アメリカの若者を中心に「カッコいい」といったニュアンスで使われています。ジャパン・クールとは、カッコいい日本、あるいは日本発のカッコいいもの、という意味になります。日本文化で海外でもっとも注目を浴びているのは、アニメやゲームの分野です。日本のアニメのクオリティの高さは世界で認められていて、ゲームの分野では「Nintendo」が一般名詞にもなっています。

さらに、日本食が海外でブームになったり、漢字のロゴが入ったＴシャツやタトゥーが人気になったりと、これまではあまり知られていなかった日本の文化が、世界の人たちに受け入れられるようになっています。

現在でもなお、日本といえば、フジヤマ、ゲイシャ、サムライ程度の認識しかない外国人もいるようですが、実際の日本について知る機会を得た外国人が増えたことで、日本独自の文化が広く理解されてきたのだと言えるでしょう。

Qなぜ、「もったいない」という日本語が脚光を浴びているのですか？

この言葉に注目したのは、ケニア出身の環境保護活動家で、2004年のノーベル平和賞受賞者であるワンガリ・マータイさんです。彼女は京都議定書関連行事で来日し

Japan and the World

■ Why has the expression "Japan cool" become popular recently?

The word "cool" has been around for quite a while, but it is still a slangy or informal expression meaning "attractive" or "impressive." "Japan cool" means that Japan itself is cool or that something from Japan is cool. The aspects of Japanese culture that attract the most attention abroad are anime and video games. Japanese anime is recognized as being of the highest quality, and in the video game sector, Nintendo is practically a household word. Even aspects of Japanese culture that, in the past, were not that well known have now become accepted worldwide, such as Japanese food or having kanji on a T-shirt or a tattoo.

Even now, there are still foreigners who know nothing more than "Fujiyama, geisha, and samurai," but as more and more foreigners are exposed to the real Japan, the unique aspects of Japanese culture have become more widely appreciated.

■ Why has the Japanese word "mottainai" suddenly received attention?

The Kenyan environmental activist Wangari Maathai, winner of the Nobel Peace Prize in 2004, brought attention to this word. When she came to Japan in connection with the Kyoto Protocol, she first heard

た際に「もったいない」という言葉を知りました。これは「あるものが、その価値を十分に発揮する前に捨てられるのはいけないことだ」というような意味です。彼女はこの言葉の意味に感銘を受け、これを世界に広めようと考えました。

そのため、マータイさんは、この言葉に該当する他言語を探しましたが、「もったいない」が持つ概念を正確に表現している単語は見つかりませんでした。そこで「もったいない」をそのまま世界共通語にすべきだと主張したのです。

これを受けて、小泉純一郎・元首相は、日本発のこの概念を広めるべくさまざまな機会に言及しています。世界的な環境保護が叫ばれる中で、「もったいない」の概念こそが解決の糸口になるとアピールしているわけです。

ただし、現実的にはまだ、マータイ氏の主張に日本が相乗りしている段階に過ぎず、実際に世界に広がっていくのはもう少し先のことになると予想されます。

Q なぜ、世界中で「カワイイ」という言葉が流行っているのですか？

海外で「カワイイ」という価値観が注目されるようになったのは、日本発のアニメやマンガ、キャラクター商品の進出が盛んになってからのことです。英語のcuteやprettyは主に人に対して使われる言葉なのに対して、日本の「カワイイ」は愛らしいもの全般に使うことができる言葉なので、海外にも受け入れられたようです。

この価値観に感銘を受けたアメリカのある有名シンガーは、歌詞のなかに「カワイイ」と入れたほか、フランスでは「カワイイ」というタイトルのテレビ番組もできています。ルノーと日産自動車のCEOであるカルロス・ゴーン氏のもとでも「カワイイ車」を研究していると言うのですから、日本的価値観が世界に認められた顕著な例だと言えるでしょう。

the word "mottainai," which could be translated as "it is too bad that this cannot be used to its full value and has to be thrown away." She was impressed with the meaning of the word and decided that the concept it represented should be known throughout the world.

She searched among other languages to see if she could find a word with a similar meaning, but she failed to find anything appropriate. She then decided that "mottaini" itself should become part of the common vocabulary of the world.

Hearing about this, then Prime Minister Junichiro Koizumi mentioned the word on a number of occasions, thinking that this Japanese concept should be more widely known. In this day and age, when the global environment is such a concern, Mr. Koizumi felt that "mottainai" could contribute to solving environmental problems.

In actuality, however, it appears that, at the present stage, Japan is simply trying to help out Dr. Maathai in her efforts to popularize the word, but it will likely take a little longer before it becomes widely known.

■ Why has the Japanese word "kawaii" become popular abroad?

It was only after anime, manga, and character goods became established abroad that the concept of "kawaii" became popular. While the English words "cute" and "pretty" are largely used in reference to people, "kawaii" can be used to describe anything that is lovely, adorable, or small and pretty. It is apparently for that reason that the word has been adopted abroad.

In the United States, a certain famous singer was so impressed by the word that she included it in the lyrics of one of her songs. In France, there is a TV program with the title Kawaii. It is said that Carlos Ghosn, CEO of Nissan and Renault, is planning a "kawaii car." From all this, you can see that "kawaii" represents an outstanding example of Japanese values being accepted overseas.

なぜ、Q 「おたく文化」は世界的になったのですか？

1980年代から使われるようになった「おたく」という言葉には、さまざまな解釈があります。時代の変遷によって、適用範囲や使用意図などに違いが見られますが、「他人とのコミュニケーションが苦手で、内向的な趣味に没頭している人たち」と言うように、侮蔑的な意味合いも含めて使われだした言葉でした。現在でも侮蔑的なニュアンスは残っていますが､言葉の適用範囲は広がり、「鉄道おたく」から「健康おたく」まで、マニアの類似語として気軽に用いられるようになっています。

「おたく」を狭義に考えたときには、アニメ、ゲーム、アイドル、美少女漫画、自作パソコンなどに没頭する人を指すことになります。海外では、日本のポピュラーカルチャー全般に興味を持つ人を指す言葉が「おたく」と受け止められているのですから、意識のズレはかなり大きいと言えるでしょう。

海外の「おたく」たちにもタイプがあり、ブックフェアやゲーム機フェアに漫画キャラクターの扮装をして集まる熱狂的な人たちから、漫画が読みたい一心で日本語を勉強する人たちまでいろいろです。どちらにしても、日本の文化に興味を持ってくれた大切なファンには違いありません。

なぜ、Q 漫画やアニメが世界を席巻したのですか？

日本の漫画やアニメが世界で注目されたのは、そのストーリー性と作画のクオリティの高さのためです。その代表的な存在が宮崎駿とスタジオジブリの作品と言えるでしょう。最初の輸出作品となった『風の谷のナウシカ』や『となりのトトロ』『もののけ姫』など、次々と出るすべての作品が好評を得て、日本アニメの地位を不動のものにしました。

ただそれより以前にも、『鉄腕アトム』や『ドラえもん』などが世界中のテレビで放映され、高い評価を受けていました。『鉄腕アトム』はアメリカでは『アストロボ

■ Why has "*otaku* culture" spread abroad?

The word "otaku" began to be used in the 1980s. Its meaning varies slightly according to the times, but at first it had the following somewhat negative meaning: "people who are bad at communicating with others and who lose themselves in hobbies that they can do without reference to other people." At present, it still retains this negative aspect, but its scope has broadened so that it can be casually used as a synonym for "freak" for "enthusiast," such as in "railroad otaku" or "fitness otaku."

In its narrow sense, "otaku" refers to people who are totally absorbed in anime, video games, pop idols, *bishōjo* (pretty underage girl) manga, homemade computers, and so on. Overseas, "otaku" refers to anyone who is interested in Japanese popular culture as a whole. So, obviously, there is quite a big difference in the understanding of the word.

Overseas, there are also different types of otaku, however. Some are complete fanatics and dress up as their favorite manga characters at book fairs and video game conventions. Others want so badly to read manga in Japanese that they start studying the language. There are other types, too, but in the end they are all enthusiastic fans of some aspect of Japanese culture.

■ Why have manga and anime become so popular throughout the world?

Japanese manga and anime have attracted a great deal of attention because of their story telling and the high quality of their artwork. The most outstanding representative of this phenomenon is the work of Hayao Miyazaki and his Studio Ghibli. From the release of his first anime, *Nausicaä of the Valley of the Wind*, to *My Neighbor Totoro*, and *Princess Mononoke*, all his work was well received, establishing the high standing of Japanese anime.

However, before that, Japanese anime such as *Astro Boy* (*Tetsuwan Atomu*), *Doraemon*, and others had been telecast on TV sta-

ーイ』というタイトルで親しまれていたのですが、「子供時代夢中になったアストロボーイが日本原作であることを大人になってから知り、自分の祖国を誇りに思った」と述懐する日系米人もいます。

なぜ、Q 日本食がブームなのですか？

日本食が海外で流行している最大の理由としては、そのヘルシーさが挙げられます。世界的に健康志向が高まってきていて、穀物や野菜を中心にした自然食を指す「マクロビオティック」という考えなどが注目を浴びています。従来の日本食は、そうした概念に近い料理だとも言えるでしょう。

アメリカの歌手マドンナが、専属の日本人シェフを雇って、子供のアレルギーを治したことも有名な話になっています。また寿司の普及によって、欧米にはなかった文化である生魚を食べる習慣も広まり、健康的だとの評価を得ています。日本人の平均寿命が長いことは世界的にも知られていて、その事実とともに、日本食の健康性が大いに注目されているわけです。

そんな風潮の中、欧米では韓国料理店や中華料理店が日本食の看板を出して営業するという事態も発生しており、農林水産省が正統な日本料理屋を認定して告知していく制度を考えました。

ところが、これには海外のマスコミが猛反発。ボイス・オブ・アメリカ（VOA）は「スシ・ポリスがやってくる」と報道し、ワシントン・ポスト紙は「テンプラだってポルトガル起源ではないか」と論じました。

農林水産省は早々とこのアイディアを取り下げましたが、こんな騒ぎが起こることも、日本食が世界中に受け入れられている証左と言えるでしょう。

tions throughout the world and had already earned an excellent reputation. One Japanese American recalls eagerly watching *Astro Boy* when he was small, but did not know then that it was made in Japan. When, as an adult, he learned where it was made, he felt very proud of the country of his ancestors.

■ Why is Japanese food enjoying such a boom overseas?

The principal reason for the popularity of Japanese food abroad is the fact that it is healthy. With more and more people throughout the world becoming health conscious, attention has focused on macrobiotics, which advocates a natural diet consisting of cereals and vegetables. The traditional Japanese diet is close to macrobiotics in general concept.

The American singer Madonna even hired a Japanese chef to cure her child of an allergy. Also, the spread of sushi in the West has led to more people eating raw fish, a custom which was previously unknown but which is now seen as healthy. Japanese people are also known for living long lives, which contributes to the belief that Japanese food is healthy.

In the midst of all this popularity, some Chinese and Korean restaurants have changed their signs to read "Japanese Food" but continue with business as usual. The Ministry of Agriculture, Forestry and Fisheries contemplated a system of accrediting true Japanese restaurants and announcing the results.

However, this idea was met with a storm of protest from mass media abroad. The Voice of America said that the Ministry was planning on sending the "sushi police," and the *Washington Post* argued that tempura came from Portugal in the first place, anyway.

The Ministry quickly gave up the idea, and this whole fuss just goes to show how widely Japanese food has been adopted throughout the world.

なぜ、Q ゴッホはあんなに浮世絵を描いたのですか？

たしかにゴッホは肖像画のバックに浮世絵版画を並べたり、版画そのものを油絵で模写したりしています。ただこれはゴッホだけに限ったことではありません。マネ、モネ、ルノアールといった印象派の画家たちのほとんどが浮世絵の影響をうけているのです。

1856年、フランスのフェリックス・ブラックモンという版画家が、日本から送られてきた陶器の箱の中から、詰め物として使われていた「北斎漫画」の画帖を見つけました。彼は北斎のデッサンの「自由さ、正確さ」に驚嘆し、それを友人であった印象派の画家たちに見せて回りました。これがきっかけとなって彼等は浮世絵に注目するようになったのです。

また1867年、1878年の２回にわたるパリ万国博覧会には日本館も作られ、浮世絵を中心とした日本の美術品のブームが起こりました。このような流れは印象派の絵画に大きな影響を与えました。

彼らは直接浮世絵を描いたというだけではありません。上から俯瞰する構図、肖像画のバックに何も描きこまない処理、鳥や虫、魚などのクローズアップなど、いままでの西洋絵画にはなかったものをとり入れるきっかけとなったのです。

■ Why did van Gogh paint so many ukiyo-e?

It is true that Vincent van Gogh inserted ukiyo-e prints into the background of his portrait paintings and that he actually made copies of them in oil. But this interest in ukiyo-e was not confined to van Gogh alone. Almost all of the Impressionist painters, including Manet, Monet, and Renoir, were influenced by ukiyo-e.

In 1856, the French etcher Félix Bracquemond came across a copy of "Hokusai Manga" prints, which had been used as packing in a box of porcelain imported from Japan. He was astounded by the freedom and accuracy of the drawings, and he took them around to show to his Impressionist friends. This kicked off Impressionist interest in ukiyo-e.

In 1867 and 1878, Japan participated in two World's Fairs in Paris and had its own pavilion. This set off the explosive interest in Japanese art objects, centered on ukiyo-e. It was this series of events that impacted so strongly on Impressionist painting.

This impact consisted not only of the Impressionists painting ukiyo-e themselves, but in their learning the techniques of the overhead view, elimination of background in portraits, close-ups of birds, insects, and fish, and much more. The Impressionists learned much from ukiyo-e that was new to Western art.

2 自然

Q なぜ、こんなに地震が多いのですか？

世界の地震のうち約10％が日本で発生しています。地球の表面は、厚さ100キロほどの岩盤で覆われていて、これをプレートといいますが、世界で13枚しかないプレートのうち４枚が日本の周囲でせめぎ合っているため、地震が多くなっているのです。

とくに首都圏やその西につながる東海地方では、プレートの押し合いによる圧力エネルギーが蓄積されているので、大地震が起きる危険性が高いと言われています。

外国人のなかには、経験のない地震に遭遇してみたいと考えて来日する人もいるようですが、とんでもありません。1995年には6434人が亡くなった阪神・淡路大震災が起きていますし、首都圏で同程度の地震が起きれば、被害はもっと大きくなると予想されています。

Q なぜ、こんなに気候の変化に富んでいるのですか？

日本の国土は狭く、アメリカの約25分の１しかありません。それでも、緯度からみれば、日本の北端と南端はアメリカの北端と南端とほぼ重なります。アメリカでも北部と南部では気候がまったく違うのですから、北海道と沖縄で気候が違ってくるのも不思議ではありません。

Nature

■ Why are there so many earthquakes?

About 10% of the world's earthquakes occur in Japan. The surface of the earth is covered by a layer of rock that reaches down to a depth of some 100 km (62 mi). This layer is divided up into individual plates that move and push against one another. There are only thirteen major plates in the world, but four of these come together around Japan. It is the movement of these plates that causes the frequent earthquakes.

At present, there is a great deal of energy building up in the plates under the Greater Tokyo Area and the Tokai region to the west (Shizuoka prefecture, Aichi prefecture, and the southern part of Gifu prefecture). The probability of a powerful earthquake occurring in this area is said to be quite high.

Some people apparently come to Japan for the chance to experience an earthquake, but this doesn't seem to be a good idea. In 1995, 6,434 people died in the Great Hanshin-Awaji Earthquake (also called the Great Hanshin Earthquake or the Kobe Earthquake), and if an earthquake of the same size hit the Tokyo area, the number of victims would be much larger.

■ Why are there such great differences in climate?

Japan is not a large country. In area it is only one twenty-fifth the size of the United States. In latitude, however, the northernmost and southernmost points of Japan approximately match those of the United States. And just as the northern and southern parts of United States have quite different climates, Hokkaido and Okinawa are also quite different. There is nothing surprising about that.

また、日本には「四季」があります。四季がはっきりするのは、中緯度に位置していて、気団の移り変わりが大きい地域です。日本はこの条件に当てはまり、夏の小笠原気団、冬のシベリア気団、春・秋の揚子江気団、梅雨のオホーツク海気団の影響を受けます。

四季のある地域では、人の情動が活発になり、経済が活性化するといわれます。なぜかといえば、自然の移り変わりが肌で感じられ、季節に応じて活動の様式が変わってくるからです。

Qなぜ、こんなに台風が来るのですか？

近年（1971～2000年）の平均では、年間約27個の台風が発生して、そのうち約3個が上陸、約11個が接近します。

日本は台風が多いという印象を持たれがちですが、アジアでは中国、フィリピンに次いで「3番目に多い国」です。韓国や北朝鮮、ベトナムなどでも台風の被害は受けているので、日本だけがとくべつ多いわけではありません。

台風とは、太平洋や南シナ海（赤道以北、東経180度～100度）で発生する最大風速が毎秒17.2メートル以上の熱帯低気圧を指しています。

東経180度より東で発生すれば、最大風速毎秒32.7メートル以上のものが「ハリケーン」とされ、マレー半島より西に進めば「サイクロン」と呼び名が変わります。世界的に見ても、その被害に悩まされているのは日本やアジアだけではないわけです。

2002年と2006年には、ハリケーンが東経180度を越えてきて、台風と呼び名が変わった例もありました。

ご購読ありがとうございました。これから出版する本の参考にさせていただきますので、下記のアンケートにご協力いただきたく、よろしくお願い申し上げます。
なお、ご記入いただいた事項を承諾なしに上記以外の目的で使用することはございません。

---

①お買い上げいただいた本の書名

(　　　　　　　　　　　　　　　　　　　　　　　　　　　　　　)

②本書をお知りになったきっかけは？

1. 新聞広告を見て(　　　　　　新聞)　2. 雑誌広告を見て(誌名　　　　　　)
3. 書店で展示物を見て　4. 書店で実物を見て
5. 人(　　　　)からすすめられて　6. 書評を見て(媒体　　　　　　)
7. インターネットで見て(サイト名　　　　　　)
8. その他(　　　　　　)

③本書をお買い求めになった動機は？(複数回答可)

1. 新聞広告　2. 雑誌広告　3. 書店の展示　4. 人からのすすめ　5. 書評
6. 書名　7. テーマに興味があった　8. あらすじを読んで　9. 表紙デザイン
10. 著者　11. 帯の文句　12. その他(　　　　　　)

④普段お読みになっている新聞、雑誌、インターネット・サイト名

新聞(　　　　　)　雑誌(　　　　　)　サイト(　　　　　)

⑤どのくらい書店を訪れますか？

毎日／週に(　)回／月に(　)回／年に(　)回

⑥どのくらい本をご購入されますか？

毎日／週に(　)冊／月に(　)冊／年に(　)冊

⑦どんな著者の本をお読みになりたいですか？

(　　　　　　　　　　　　　　　　　　　　　　　　　　　　　　)

⑧どんなテーマ・内容の本をお読みになりたいですか？

(　　　　　　　　　　　　　　　　　　　　　　　　　　　　　　)

⑥本書のご感想

(　　　　　　　　　　　　　　　　　　　　　　　　　　　　　　)

ご感想をHPや広告等に匿名でご紹介させていただいてもよろしいですか？

□ 可 ・ □ 不可

郵便はがき

料金受取人払

牛込局承認

5081

差出有効期間
平成20年3月
31日まで

162-8790

東京都新宿区新小川町
9番25号 5F

ランダムハウス講談社 行

●お名前	●生年月日 19 年 月 日生	●性別 男・女
●Eメール @		
●ご住所 〒 都道府県		
●ご職業 1. 会社員 2. 経営者 3. 公務員 4. 自営業 5. 教職 6. 主婦 7. 学生 8. フリーター 9. 無職 10. その他（ ）		
●ご購入店 区市町村 店	●ご購入日 月頃	

今後、ランダムハウス講談社から各種ご案内などをお送りしてもよろしいでしょうか。
ご承諾いただける方は、右の□に○をご記入ください。 □

In addition, Japan has four distinct seasons. The reason for this is that Japan is located, for the most part, in the northern middle latitudes, and is affected by the movement of a number of air masses. In summer there is the Ogasawara air mass; in winter the Siberia air mass; in spring and autumn the so-called Yangze air mass; and the Sea of Okhotsk air mass that affects the rainy season.

It is often said that in regions where there are four distinct seasons, people tend to be mentally and physically alert, resulting in greater economic activity. The reason is that the changing seasons have a direct impact on the body, and people change their pattern of living to suit each season.

■ Why are there so many typhoons in Japan?

From 1971 to 2000, there have been an average of twenty-seven typhoons every year. About three of those typhoons reached land (made landfall), and about eleven approached land.

It may seem that Japan has a ralatively large number of typhoons, but in fact, Japan is number three behind China and the Philippines among Asian countries. North Korea, South Korea, and Vietnam are also visited by typhoons, so it cannot be said that Japan is particularly special in this regard.

Tropical depressions that originate in the Pacific Ocean and the South China Sea (between 180 degrees east and 100 degrees east longitude) are called typhoons if they have a speed of over 17.2 meters per second (38 miles per hour).

Tropical depressions that originate east of 180 degrees and have a speed of over 32.7 meters per second (72 miles per hour) are called hurricanes; however, if they move west of the Malay Peninsula, they are called cyclones. Thus, from a global perspective, it is not only Japan and other East Asian countries that suffer from such storms.

As far as the naming goes, in 2002 and 2006 there were cases in which hurricanes crossed 180 degrees east longitude and were therefore renamed typhoons.

なぜ、Q 富士山はあんなに均整がとれた姿をしているのですか？

「フジヤマ、ゲイシャ、シンカンセン」……。シンカンセンの代わりには「ゼン」「スシ」「ハラキリ」「クロサワ」などと、様々な言葉が入ってくることもありますが、フジヤマとゲイシャは、外国人から見た日本のイメージの代表格になっているようです。もちろん、日本ではフジヤマではなく富士山（ふじさん）と呼びますが、日本人にとっても、美しきシンボルであるのは間違いありません。

日本で富士山に似ている山は、そこの地名に富士を付けた愛称で呼ばれます。たとえば北海道の羊蹄山は「蝦夷富士」と呼ばれます。蝦夷とは北海道の古称です。こうした「郷土富士」は日本全国で300以上存在しています。

ただし、海に面していて、海抜0メートルから標高3776メートルまで円錐形にそそり立つ雄大な姿は富士山ならではのものでしょう。標高が高いために山頂が雪に覆われていることも美しさをひきたてています。古くから信仰の対象になり、絵画のモチーフにもなっているように、やはり富士山の存在感には、他を圧倒する絶対的なものがあります。

これまで何度かの噴火活動によって現在の形が作られてきたのですから、「休火山」である富士山がまた噴火する危険は否定できません。最近の大爆発は1707年でしたが、それから300年が経過しています。新たな大爆発が起きれば、その姿がさらに変わってしまう可能性もあるわけです。

■ Why does Mt. Fuji have such a symmetrical shape?

It seems that Fujiyama, geisha, and the shinkansen (or bullet train) are considered by many foreigners to be symbols of Japanese culture. The shinkansen is sometimes replaced by another word, such as zen or sushi or harakiri or Kurosawa, but Fujiyama and geisha retain their status as the most common Japanese symbols among foreigners. Of course, Japanese say Fujisan rather than Fujiyama, but in any case even Japanese consider Mt. Fuji to be a symbol of the country.

Japanese mountains that resemble Mt. Fuji are sometimes given a nickname, in which cases the name of the place where it is located is followed by "Fuji." For example, the mountain in Hokkaido that is officially called Yoteizan has the nickname "Ezo Fuji," "Ezo" being an older name for Hokkaido. There are over 300 such local Fujis throughout Japan.

However, Mt. Fuji is the only one that faces the sea, rises to 3,776 meters (12,388 ft) above sea level, and has such a beautiful cone shape. The peak of the mountain is often covered in snow, which adds to its beauty. From olden times, Mt. Fuji has been considered sacred, and has served as a motif in many paintings and other works of art. Undeniably, Mt. Fuji has a presence unique among mountains.

The present shape is the result of many eruptions, and even though it is now inactive, there is still a possibility of further eruptions. The last big eruption occurred in 1707, some 300 years ago. If Mt. Fuji should erupt again in the future, its all-to-familiar shape might change.

なぜ、Q

■なぜ、こんなに島が多いのですか？

外国人は、「日本は主として本州、北海道、九州、四国という４つの島で形成されている」と認識していることも多いようですが、日本人はこの４島を島だとは認識していません。これらは日本の国土の中心になっているので、この４島以外のものからはじめて島だと意識しています。

日本は6852の島で形成されていますが、この数字を知っている日本人はあまりいません。そもそも日本は「日本列島」を国土にしているわけですが、列島と言われてはじめて、本州や北海道も島だった、と思い出すのが大半の日本人です。

日本になぜ島が多いかといえば、これもプレートと関係していて、地殻の浮き沈みの影響を受けるためです。プレートの境界域では列島が形成されやすいのです。

■ Why does Japan have so many islands?

Most foreigners think of Japan as being formed by the four islands of Honshu, Hokkaido, Kyushu, and Shikoku. Oddly enough, Japanese don't think of these four as being islands at all. They think of them as simply being the core, or the main body, of the nation of Japan. Aside from these four, there are many other islands, and it is these islands that Japanese generally think of as being real islands.

In fact, Japan is made up of 6,852 islands, although not many Japanese are aware of it. Japan is, without a doubt, an archipelago, but most Japanese don't think of the four main islands as being part of a group of islands until they actually hear the word "archipelago."

As to why there are so many islands, this is due to the crust of the earth rising and falling according to the movement of the tectonic plates around Japan. Islands are easily formed along the boundaries of these plates.

3 文化

Q なぜ、

茶道や華道には「道」が付いているのですか？

まず「道」という漢字から説明しなければいけないでしょう。この漢字は１字だけだと「みち」と読みますが、他の語の後ろについたときは「どう」と発音されます。この字にはふたつの意味があって、まず第１の意味は実際に歩く道のことです。そして第２の意味は自分の精神をより高いものにするために歩く、精神の道といったものです。このため、何かをする技術をみがくためだけではなく、それを通して精神も高めようとするものに対して「道」という言葉がつきます。

それではお茶を飲むことや生け花にどうして「道」がつくのでしょう。お茶を飲む習慣は、禅宗とともに中国から持ち込まれ、やがて村田珠光（1423-1502）という室町時代の僧によって茶道の原型がつくられました。

一方、花を活ける習慣は古くからありましたが、やはり室町時代に、京都・六角堂の僧侶が、お寺の本尊である如意輪観音に花を供えていたことから華道の原型が体系化したといわれています。

つまり、茶道にしても華道にしても、それぞれに仏教との結びつきがあり、それも関係して「精神修養」としての意味合いを強く持っているのです。

華道には「生け花」という言い方もあります。また茶道は「茶の湯」とも言います。このふたつを通して技術だけではなく精神修養もするとき、それを強調するために「道」を付けるのです。

■ Why are the tea ceremony (*sadō*) and flower arranging (*kadō*) referred to as "paths" or "ways" (*dō*)?

The important thing here is to explain that the Chinese character 道 is pronounced *michi* when standing alone, and *dō* when used as a suffix. It can be translated as "way," "path," or "road," and it has two meanings. First it means a physical road or path that one travels down. The second meaning is a "way" to improve oneself spiritually. *Michi* or *dō* is used when some activity is seen not just as a technical or practical matter but as a matter of the heart or spirit.

So how did *dō* come to be attached to the art of arranging flowers or of drinking tea? The custom of drinking tea first entered Japan from China along with Zen Buddhism. In the Muromachi period (1333-1568) the Buddhist priest Murata Shukō formulated the basic principles of the tea ceremony as a spiritual undertaking, as a *michi* or *dō*: "The Way of Tea."

As for flower arrangement, the simple act of arranging flowers had been practiced in Japan from olden times. However, again in the Muromachi period, a priest at the Rokkakudō temple, Kyoto, elevated this simple custom to a spiritual practice. While arranging flowers at the temple, he worked out the basic principles behind the "path" of arranging flowers: "The Way of Flowers."

So, both tea and flower arranging had a connection with Buddhism, and this is undoubtedly how they came to take on a spiritual significance. Flower arranging can be called ikebana ("arranging flowers") instead of *kadō*, and the tea ceremony can be referred to as *cha no yu* ("the water of tea") instead of *sadō*. But when you want to emphasize the spiritual side of these two activities, you should say *kadō* (The Way of Flowers) and *sadō* (The Way of Tea).

なぜ、Q 「わび・さび」を大切にするのですか？

「わび・さび」とふたつを括って用いられるケースが増えていますが、本来、「侘（わび）」と「寂（さび）」は別の概念です。

わびとは、もともと「立派な状態に対する劣った状態」を指していて、日本美術をアメリカに紹介した明治時代の美術評論家・岡倉天心は、わびを「imperfect（不完全なもの）」と訳しています。その一方、さびは「時間の経過で朽ちていくさま」を指しているので、わび・さびともにネガティブな意味を持つ言葉だとも言えるでしょう。

中世の茶人、千利休（1522-1591）は、無駄や華美を省いて、禁欲主義的な価値観を持つ「わび茶」という様式を作りました。その中で彼は、わびを、貧しさの中にある豊かさ、簡素さの中にある美しさという肯定的な概念に変えたのです。

たとえば茶室に飾る花は、西洋のフラワーアレンジメントのように豪華な色と形の組み合わせで人の心をひきつけようとするものではなく、たった1本の花を小さな花器に投げ入れただけで自然を象徴させ、茶室の中で自然そのものを感じさせようとしています。

一方のさびは、いってみればアンティーク趣味とも近いところがあるのかもしれません。古びて朽ちていく中に味わいを見出す感覚こそが、さびだとも言えるでしょう。

ただ、アンティークを収集する際には「この品物は何百年前につくられた珍しいものだ」などと考える場合も多いでしょう。しかし、さびにおいては、そうした歴史的価値や商品的価値は問われません。

時間の流れとともに自然に醸し出される変化そのものに対し、あくまで個人的に何を感じるかが問われてくるのです。

■ Why are *wabi* and *sabi* so important?

The words *wabi* and *sabi* are used to refer to two particularly Japanese ways of looking at art and the world. Recently, these two concepts have often been combined as if they were one thing—*wabi-sabi*—but they are actually two different concepts.

Wabi is used to describe things that appear to be inferior or lacking, in contrast to things that appear magnificent and flawless. When the critic Tenshin Okakura first introduced Japanese art to the United States in the Meiji period (1868-1912), he translated *wabi* as "imperfect." On the other hand, *sabi* describes things that, with the passage of time, have gone through some change that shows their age. You could say that both words have something negative about them.

The tea master Sen no Rikyū (1522-1591) developed a type of tea ceremony from which he removed everything that wasn't essential as well as all elements of display. He called it *wabi* tea (*wabi cha*). In the Spartan environment he created for this type of tea ceremony, he discovered a special kind of richness; in its simplicity, he discovered a special beauty. What he had done was turn the negative elements of *wabi* into positive elements.

For instance, the floral arrangement in the tea room was not a grand affair with many combinations of colors and shapes such as you might find in the West. Rather it was a single flower placed in a smallish vase in an almost casual manner. This single flower was just as effective as a larger display in bringing nature into the tea room.

Sabi can be said to have something in common with the appreciation of antiques. Finding beauty in what is growing old and faded is what *sabi* is about.

However, antique collectors might also be interested in precisely how old or rare something is. An object's historical or commercial value, however, is not part of the spirit of *sabi*.

Sabi is concerned solely with the individual's appreciation of the changes that naturally appear with the passage of time.

Qなぜ、小さなものが好きなのですか？

盆栽や箱庭などは「ミニチュア文化」とも呼ばれています。韓国の初代文化相で評論家の李御寧氏が1980年代に『「縮み」志向の日本人』というベストセラーを出しました。この本の中で彼は、“日本人は拡大するものには弱いのに、縮小するものに向かうと非常に才能を発揮する”ということを指摘し、これが日本の文化の特徴のひとつであり、工業の発達とも関連していると主張しました。

たしかに、古来、「美しい」という言葉には「小さい」という意味が含まれていたとも考えられているので、日本人は小さなものに愛情を感じ、精巧なものに感嘆する傾向があるのでしょう。手先が器用なため、そうしたものを作り出すのに適していたのかもしれません。

1本の木の中に自然全体を表現するような盆栽を作ったり、幕の内弁当のように、いろいろな味を小さな箱につめ込んだりする発想が、トランジスターを作ったり、ウォークマンを作ったりするのに共通しているのだ、と李御寧氏は言います。

Qなぜ、こんなに桜が好きなのですか？

桜は、厳しい冬を越して春を迎えたときに一気に咲いて、1週間ほどで花を散らせます。「花は桜木、人は武士」とも言われますが、その潔いありようは、戦場で死を怖れない武士の理想とも重ねられてきました。ほんの一時だけの美しさは、「もののあわれ」を感じさせるものであり、武士に限らず日本人すべての心をとらえてきたのです。

平安時代の歌人・西行（1118-1190）は、「願はくは花の下にて春死なん　そのきさらぎの望月のころ」とも詠んでいます。この花とは桜のことですが、桜が咲く季節は、それだけ特別なものになっています。

■ Why do Japanese like small things?

Bonsai and *hakoniwa* (gardens in a small box) are examples of Japanese miniaturization. In his bestselling book *Smaller Is Better: Japan's Mastery of the Miniature*, O-Young Lee makes the point that while Japanese are not especially good at making large things, they are very good at making small things. He says that this is a characteristic of Japanese culture that is related to the development of Japanese industry.

It is true that the Japanese word for "beauty" (*utsukushii*) originally included the meaning of "small." Japanese do seem to love small things and admire anything that shows fine and delicate workmanship. Since Japanese are fairly clever with their hands, they are suited to making such objects.

O-Young Lee cites a number of examples of Japanese miniaturization, including the bonsai, where one small tree stands as a representation of all nature, and the boxed lunch (*maku-no-uchi bentō*), in which a number of tasty foods are packed in a small box. In modern times, this talent for miniaturization led to the development of transistors, Walkmans, and much more.

■ Why are Japanese so fond of cherry blossoms?

The cherry tree blooms all at once just as winter has come to an end and spring has arrived. Then, within a week's time, it loses all its blossoms. There is an old saying, "Among trees, the cherry is best; among people, the samurai." The way the cherry suddenly blooms, and just as suddenly loses all its petals, is thought to be similar to the samurai ideal of going into battle without fear or the slightest hesitation. The fact that cherry blossoms show their beauty for such a short time appeals to the Japanese sense of the fragility of life; not just samurai, of course, but all Japanese.

The poet Saigyō (1118-1190) has left us a poem about the cherry blossoms that shows how special that season of the year is:

日本では、欧米と違い、ちょうど桜の咲く時期が入学や入社の時期と重なることもあり、華やかなスタートのイメージにもなります。その春のウキウキした気分を楽しみ、また花の一瞬の美しさをめでるために、桜の下で「お花見」という宴会を催します。

また、日本の桜といえばソメイヨシノという品種が中心で、一度に咲き、一度に散ってしまいますが、最近は開花期間が違う桜を植えて、長い期間楽しもうという動きも出てきています。桜に対する接し方、感じ方も変わってきているのかもしれません。

Qなぜ、日本庭園の松は、曲がりくねっているのですか？

日本の庭園は、海外の庭園のような広大な空間にするのではなく、小さいけれども庭全体で何かを表現しようとしている場合がほとんどです。その基本となるのは「縮景」という発想で、自然の景色を庭の中に縮めて、山や海や川などを映し出そうとしています。そうしたなかでは、池をつくって、それを海に見立てるといったわかりやすい方法だけでなく、砂によって海を模写するなど、さまざまな方法がとられています。

そうして、庭全体が自然を模写しているだけでなく、庭の中の松の木１本にも自然のイメージを求めます。その自然さを出すために、針金で枝を固定してわざと曲げたり、周囲に岩を配置するなど、知恵を絞った技巧が凝らされているのです。

Dying under the cherries in spring,
A full moon above, in the second month—
What more could one want.

Different from Europe and the United States, the cherry blossom season coincides with the beginning of the new school year and the start of new jobs for recently hired employees. Therefore the season also has a bright, lively image suggesting new beginnings in life. People enjoy this happy atmosphere, admire the cherry blossoms, and take part in "flower-viewing" parties under the cherry trees. It is a special time of year.

There are several hundred types of cherry trees in Japan, but the most highly regarded is the *Somei Yoshino*, which suddenly blooms and just as suddenly looses its blossoms, as described above. Recently some people have been planting varieties that bloom at slightly different times, hoping to lengthening the total time of the experience. The feeling toward cherry blossoms may be undergoing a change.

■ Why do the pine trees in Japanese gardens have such odd shapes?

Most Japanese gardens are not the huge spaces you might find in other countries, but small spaces that try to express something large. The main principle behind Japanese gardens is the miniaturized landscape. The natural landscape is brought into the garden in a downsized form, and mountains and rivers are recreated. There are simple techniques like having a pond represent the sea, but there are also other, more sophisticated techniques, such as creating ocean-like patterns in sand.

While it is true that the garden as a whole is a representation of nature, each element in the garden—each pine tree—can also be an expression of nature. In order to show the pine tree as it might exist in nature, for example, wire is wrapped around its branches to give them a wind-blown shape. Many different techniques are used to create such natural impressions.

4 日本語

Qなぜ、

日本語には３種類もの書き方があるのですか？

日本語を表記するには３種類の文字が使われます（さらにローマ字が用いられることもあります）。

もともと日本語には文字がありませんでした。そのため、本来は表意文字である漢字の音だけを借りるかたちで、表音文字として漢字を使用する方法が採られるようになりました。

しかし、字画の多い漢字をアルファベットのように使っていくのは大変なので、漢字を崩したり、漢字の一部を利用して音を表すようにしました。この漢字を崩したのが平仮名で、一部を利用したのが片仮名なのです。

現在では、重要な単語や動詞などは漢字を中心に表記して、補助的な助詞や副詞などには平仮名を使い、海外から入ってきた言葉などには片仮名を使うようになっています。

漢字を崩して作った平仮名は、平安時代(794-1185)の女性たちが中心となって使ったものです。ここから『源氏物語』や『枕草子』という名作が生まれました。そして漢字の一部を使って作ったのが片仮名で、これは漢文を使う男性、主として経典を読む僧侶によって作られました。

The Japanese Language

■ Why does the Japanese writing system have three different scripts?

There are three ways to write Japanese; that is, Japanese has three different scripts. In addition to these three scripts, sometimes the Latin alphabet is also used.

At the very beginning, Japanese had no writing system. To create one, Japanese borrowed Chinese characters, or kanji. Kanji were primarily meant to represent meaning (and only secondarily sound) and are therefore often called ideograms. Japanese gradually came to use kanji for their sound alone.

But because kanji were not easy to write (because of the number of strokes it took to write one character), they were not as convenient as an alphabet in representing sound. So the next step was to simplify the kanji by, first, making them more cursive (that is, writing them so the different parts ran together and reduced the number of individual strokes); and second, by taking one part of the kanji and isolating it so that it became independent and represented one sound. The cursive style resulted in what is called *hiragana*, and the one-part style resulted in what is called *katakana*.

In Japanese today, important words like verbs and nouns are usually written in kanji. Secondary words like particles and adverbs are written in hiragana. Loan words (that is, foreign words that have been adopted into the Japanese language) are written in katakana.

Hiragana was developed in the Heian period (794-1185), mostly by women. Literary masterpieces such as *The Tale of Genji* and *The Pillow Book*, both written by women, were created during this period. Katakana (the script created from one part of a kanji) was mostly developed by men who wrote in kanji or by Buddhist monks

なぜ、同じ漢字に２通りの読み方があるのですか？

ほとんどの日本の漢字には訓読みと音読みというふたつの読み方があります。日本古来の言い方が訓読みで、中国風の発音が音読みです。

これは、中国の文字である漢字を使って日本語を表そうとした事情から出たものです。

たとえば「いぬ」という動物を文字で書くとき、中国では同じ動物を「犬」という字で書いていたので、それをそのまま借りてきて、「いぬ」と読むようにしました。これが訓読みです。ところが、中国ではこの文字を「けん」と発音していたのでそれも使うようになりました。これが音読みです。

このため「この犬（いぬ）は日本犬（けん）です」というようにふたつの読み方ができてしまったのです。

仮に、漢字ではなく英語が入ってきていたなら、「dog」と書いて「いぬ」と読むのが訓読みで、「ドッグ」と読むのが音読みということになっていたわけです。

なぜ、「つまらないもの」をプレゼントするのですか？

日本語には「敬語」という表現法があり、日本語の特徴のひとつになっているのですが、これが日本語学習者を悩ませています。とくに学習者の母語にこのような表現がないとタイヘンです。とはいっても、実は日本人にとっても敬語はやっかいなものなのです。

敬語を大別すると、尊敬語、謙譲語、丁寧語の３つに分かれますが、「つまらないもの」というのは謙譲語に

who used the katakana as aids in their readings of Chinese-language sutras.

■ Why can an individual kanji be read in more than one way?

Most kanji (Chinese characters) have at least two readings (that is, two ways they can be pronounced). One is the Japanese way (called *kun-yomi*), and the other is the Chinese way (*on-yomi*).

This situation came about because of Japan's adoption of Chinese characters to write the Japanese language. Let's say that a Japanese person wanted to write "dog." He or she would see that a Chinese character already existed for writing dog, and he should use that character, pronouncing it in the Japanese way: *inu*. But at the same time this person would notice that the Chinese had their own way of pronouncing that character, which is *ken*.

Now let's say this person wanted to say, "This dog is a Japanese dog." According to the context of the sentence, the first character for "dog" would be read in the Japanese way as *inu*, and the second "dog" would be read in the Chinese way as *ken*. So the sentence would read like this: "This *inu* is a Japanese *ken*."

If you wanted to, you could do the same thing with Japanese and English instead of Japanese and Chinese. The English word "dog" would be pronounced by Japanese speakers as "doggu," however. So the sentence would read, "This *inu* is a Japanese *doggu*."

■ Why do Japanese say, "This is the merest trifle," when giving someone a gift?

Honorific language is one of the chief characteristics of the Japanese language. It is also one of the more difficult aspects for foreign students (particularly if their own language does not have something similar). But, if the truth be known, Japanese also find honorific language troublesome at times.

Honorific language can be divided into three categories: respect-

あたります。謙譲語というのは、自分あるいは身内、自分の所有物などを卑下して表現することによって相手を一段高いものと感じさせるものです。

最近は用いられることが減りつつありますが、「拙者」（つたない者＝自分）、「愚妻」（愚かな妻＝自分の妻）、豚児（豚のような児＝自分の子供）といった言葉もあります。

これらの言葉の意味を英語に訳せば、聞いた相手は驚くでしょうが、これを使っている日本人も、それを聞いた日本人も、意味そのものは本気で捉えていません。あくまで、自分や妻、子供などを控えめに言うための単語として使用しているだけだからです。ただ、当人たちの前ではあまり使わない方がいいでしょう……。

同じように、日本人は人に何かをプレゼントする際に「つまらないものですが」と言いながら渡すことがありますが、本当につまらないものだと考えていることはまずありません。自分の妻のことを本気で「愚か」だとは考えていないのと同じです。

Qなぜ、電話に出たときに「もしもし」と言うのですか？

日本で電話が使われるようになったばかりの頃、「もしもし」と言って話し始めていたことから、この言葉が残りました。この「もしもし」は「申し、申し（話します、話します）」を縮めた呼びかけの言葉であるとされています。つまり、電話をかけた人は、出た相手に、これから話しますよと伝えているのです。このため、受け手側が「もしもし」で始めるのはおかしいとして、ビジネス・マナーでは「もしもしとは言わないように」と教育されます。

また、「もしもし」は、英語の「ハロー」に似たニュアンスの聞き返しの言葉として用いられることもあります。電話が使われるようになったばかりの頃には、自分の言葉が相手に伝わっているかという不安から「もしも

ful language, humble language, and polite language. Referring to something as the "merest trifle" is an example of humble language. By using humble language in reference to yourself or to things connected with you, you lower or devalue yourself while elevating the other person to a higher status.

There are many other examples of humble expressions, though it is true that they are becoming less common these days. For example, *sessha* ("awkward fellow" = "I"), *gusai* ("foolish wife" = "my wife"), and *tonji* ("pig child" = "my child").

Naturally, if you think of the literal meaning of these words, it may seem a bit shocking, but in reality the Japanese speaking these words, as well as the Japanese being spoken to, aren't thinking of the literal meaning. They simply accept the words as being humble references to oneself, one's wife, or one's child. It might be best, however, not to use these expressions in front of the person being referred to.

In the same way, as they hand a gift to someone, a Japanese might say, "This is the merest trifle," but they don't seriously believe that it is a trifle. The same applies to their "foolish wife."

■ Why do Japanese say *moshi moshi* when they answer the phone?

When telephones first came into use in Japan, people began conversations by saying *moshi moshi*, and this custom has survived to the present. It is said that this first *moshi moshi* was actually a shortened form of *mōshi*, *mōshi*, which means "I will speak, I will speak." It was a way of calling out to the other party to let them know you were ready to speak. Since it would be somewhat odd if the person on the receiving end also said, "I will speak, I will speak," it became an accepted business practice for the receiver not to repeat the phrase.

However, another function of *moshi moshi* is to check to see if the other party is still on the line and listening. In that sense it might be similar to English "Hello" when the other party hasn't said any-

し」と呼びかけていたので、その名残りだともいわれています。

なお、アメリカで電話が実用化されたばかりの頃、第一声の呼びかけの言葉として、電話の発明者アレクサンダー・グラハム・ベルは「Ahoy」（船員が他船に呼びかける言葉）を考えましたが、友人のトマス・エジソンが「Hello」の方がいいと提案して、これが一般化したとされています。

Qなぜ、日本人は英語が苦手なのですか？

日本では、常日頃から英語を話す機会がほとんどないということが第一の理由として挙げられます。また、たとえば英語とドイツ語などでは、文法や単語、文字などに共通点、類似点が多いのにくらべ、英語と日本語には共通点はほとんどありません。

さらに、英語の発音は子音が中心であるのに対して日本の発音は母音が中心であるため、音としても馴染みにくいという問題も挙げられます。

そして、もうひとつよく指摘されることは教育方針の問題です。日本では、高校受験、大学受験などが非常に大きな意味を持っているため、ペーパーテストの点数が重要視されます。

そのため文法と読解の教育に重点が置かれ、採点しにくい聞き取りや発音に関しては軽視されてきたのです。そのため、ほとんど英語の会話はできなくても、英語で書かれている本を読むことはできるという人もいるわけです。

もともと日本人の教養というのは、中国の古典を学ぶことでしたが、中国語を読むことと書くことはできても、話すこと、聞くことはまったくできなかったのです。これは欧米の人がラテン語を学ぶのと同じようなものかもしれません。

こんな時代が1500～1600年間も続きました。そして明治時代（1868-1912）になって英語を学ぶことが主

thing for a while and you want to make sure they are still there. One theory is that *moshi moshi* actually originated in this way, from the fear that the other party might not be hearing what you were saying.

Incidentally, when the telephone first came into use in the United States, its inventor, Alexander Graham Bell, thought that the right word to begin a telephone call should be "Ahoy," the expression used when calling out to a ship. But his friend Thomas Edison suggested "Hello," and that became the general practice.

■ Why are Japanese so bad at English?

First, there are just too few opportunities to speak English while in Japan. Second, English and Japanese have very little in common as languages, unlike English and German, for example, which are similar in grammar, vocabulary, and writing system.

Further, English pronunciation lays emphasis on consonants while Japanese emphasizes vowels, meaning that Japanese speakers have trouble getting used to the English way of pronouncing words.

Also, there is the problem of education policy, an issue which is often pointed out. Since high school and university entrance exams are given top priority, the scores that students get on paper-and-pencil tests are seen as very important.

For that reason, emphasis is laid on grammar and reading ability, while listening and pronunciation, which are hard to score anyway, are given less attention. As a result, there are quite a few people who can read English books but find it almost impossible to carry on a conversation in English.

In the past, getting an education meant reading Chinese classics. Still, even though people could read and write Chinese, they were completely unable to speak it. This may be similar to Westerners learning Latin.

This situation continued for 1,500 to 1,600 years. At the beginning of the Meiji period (1868-1912), when English became the principal foreign language to learn, the emphasis was again placed on reading, just as it had been with Chinese. This history helps explain

流になったときにも、同じように読むことに重点がおかれました。日本人が外国語の学び方がヘタなのにはこうした歴史的背景もあるのです。
ともあれ、英語の成績はアジア各国の中でも最低に近いので、現在は中学校から始めている英語教育を、小学校から始めようとしているところです。

Qなぜ、こんなにたくさん和製英語があるのですか？

ハンドル = steering wheel、バックミラー = rear-view mirror、アフターサービス = customer serviceなど、英語より英語らしい？単語が日本語にはあります。
こんな和製英語にはいくつかのパターンがあって、上に挙げた例は、本当の英語が日本人にとってはわかりにくい、あるいは言いにくいというものでしょう。
それからセクハラ = sexual harassment、パソコン = personal computer、コンビニ = convenience storeというように単語の頭の部分だけをとって作りあげたものがあります。
またベッドタウン = bedroom suburbs、ゴールイン = reach the goal、モーニングサービス = morning specialといったように、乏しい語彙を勝手な英語感覚でつなぎあわせたものもあります。
このように和製英語にもいくつかのタイプがありますが、すべてカタカナで書かれ、外国起源の言葉であることを示しています。

why Japanese are not very good at foreign languages.

In any case, Japan is at the bottom of the class among Asian countries when it comes to English proficiency. As a result, there is now a movement to start teaching English in elementary schools, instead of junior high schools as it is done now.

■ Why is there so much Japanese English?

English "steering wheel" = Japanese *handoru* ("handle"). English "rearview mirror" = Japanese *bakku mirā* ("back mirror"). English "customer service" = Japanese *afutā sābisu* ("after service"). These are a few examples of English expressions created in Japan; some of them not all that bad.

Japanese English comes in a number of different forms. The examples given above were probably created because the real English was either hard to understand or difficult to pronounce.

Here are some examples in which the beginnings of two words (or of one word in the last example) were combined to create a new word. English "sexual harassment" = Japanese *sekuhara*. English "personal computer" = Japanese *pasokon*. English "convenience store" = Japanese *konbini*.

Sometimes words are just thrown together in an English-like fashion to make up for a lack of proper vocabulary. English "bedroom suburb" = Japanese *beddo taun* ("bed town"). English "reach a goal" = Japanese *gōruin* ("goal in"). English "morning special" = Japanese *mōningu sābisu* ("morning service").

While there are a number of different types of words like this, all of them are written in *katakana* to show their foreign origin.

5 健康・身体

Q なぜ、日本人は長生きなのですか？

2006年の世界保健機関（ＷＨＯ）の発表によれば、日本人の平均寿命は82歳で、モナコ、サンマリノと並んで世界１位になっています。男女別に見ても、男性が78.64歳でアイスランドに次いで世界２位、女性は85.59歳で単独世界１位です。ただ、日本でも19世紀中頃には平均寿命は30歳台で、20世紀初頭は40歳前後だったと言われています。戦後の復興が軌道に乗ったあと、急激に平均寿命が伸びていったのです。

その理由はいくつか挙げられますが、ひとつには新生児死亡率の低さがあります。新生児1000人当たりの死亡数は、最近（2000～2005年）の統計で3.2人となっており、これは先進国のなかでももっとも少ない数字です。そのほかの要因としては、医療制度の確立や食生活の改善などが挙げられます。伝統的な日本食は、低脂肪、低カロリーでしたが、その欠点とされる低動物性蛋白と高食塩が改善されて、栄養学的に見てもバランスがとれた食生活になっているのです。

Q なぜ、肥満が少ないのですか？

肥満の基準が一定化してないこともあり、数値の比較は難しいのですが、世界の中でもアメリカの肥満率はかなり高く、韓国や中国、インド、日本などが低いとされています。標準体重を上回るという意味では、アメリカ人は２人に１人、日本人は５人に１人程度が肥満だとも

Health and Physical Characteristics

■ Why do Japanese live so long?

According to a 2006 report issued by the World Health Organization (WHO), the average Japanese life span is 82 years old, tying with Monaco and San Marino for first place. In terms of gender, Japanese men, at age 78.64, are second behind Iceland. At 85.59 years, women have the longest life span in the world. In the mid nineteenth century, however, the average Japanese life span was in the mid thirties, and at the beginning of the twentieth century it was around forty. It was only after economic recovery from the war had seriously begun that the average life span increased dramatically.

There are several reasons for this sudden increase. One is the low rate of infant mortality. From 2000 to 2005, the Japanese infant mortality rate was 3.2 per 1,000. Among industrially advanced nations, this is by far the lowest rate. Other reasons include the establishment of a modern medical system and dietary improvements. The traditional Japanese diet is low in fat and low in calories, but it is also low in animal protein and high in salt. From a nutritional point of view, the modern Japanese diet is quite balanced.

■ Why are there so few obese (overweight) people in Japan?

First of all, the definition of obesity is not fixed, and it is difficult to compare different obesity rates. Still, it can be said that the rate of obesity is high in the United States and low in South Korea, China, India, and Japan. If obesity is defined as weighing more than one's

言われています。これはやはり、食生活の影響が大きいものと考えられます。アメリカ人の食事が高カロリーなのに対し、日本やアジアの食事は低カロリーにおさえられています。

ただ、日本でも最近、「メタボリック症候群」が問題視されています。肥満の人が、高血圧、高血糖、高脂血症のうち2つ以上に該当するとメタボリック症候群と判定されて、脳卒中や心筋梗塞になる危険が指摘されます。予備軍まで合わせれば、40歳以上の男性の50％以上、女性の約20％が該当するという調査結果も出ています。

Q なぜ、すぐに酔っ払うのですか？

アルコールで酔った状態になるのは、アセトアルデヒドが神経や血管に影響を与えるからですが、このアセトアルデヒドを作るアルコール脱水素酵素（ADH）が日本人の約80％の場合、異型であるため、アセトアルデヒドを早く作りすぎるとされています。そのため、早く酔って、酔いがさめにくくなっているのです。

これは遺伝の問題なので、生まれつきお酒に弱い人が大半というわけです。それにもかかわらず、お酒が好きな人は多いので、街頭や電車の中で酔った人が見られるということになります。

Q なぜ、メガネをかけた人が多いのですか？

昔から欧米人は、イラストや映画などで「メガネ、出っ歯、カメラ」を日本人の特徴として描いてきました。日本人のメガネ使用率はたしかに高く、約30～40％と

ideal weight, then one out of every two Americans is obese, and about one out of five Japanese. The biggest factor is diet. Americans tend to have a high calorie diet, while Japanese and other East Asians have a lower calorie diet.

Recently, however, metabolic syndrome has become a problem in Japan. Metabolic syndrome means that the person is at risk of stroke or heart attack. If an obese person has two of the three following symptoms—high blood pressure, hyperglycemia (excessive glucose or sugar in the blood), hyperlipemia (excessive fat in the blood)—he or she is diagnosed as having metabolic syndrome. According to some reports, if those who are just short of having metabolic syndrome are counted, then over 50 percent of Japanese men over forty and about 20 percent of women over forty would be considered in danger.

■ Why do Japanese tend to get drunk (intoxicated) rather quickly?

An intoxicated condition is produced by the effect of the chemical acetaldehyde on the nerves and blood vessels in the body. In about 80 percent of Japanese, the substance (alcohol dehydrogenase) that produces acetaldehyde is abnormal, resulting in excessive amounts of acetaldehyde being quickly produced. Consequently, most Japanese become easily intoxicated (drunk) and are slow to recover from it.

This is a matter of genetics, and therefore most Japanese are never able to drink large amounts of alcohol. Still, many of these people like drinking alcoholic beverages anyway, and that is why we see so many drunks in the streets and on trains.

■ Why do so many Japanese wear glasses?

Traditionally, Westerners have depicted Japanese in cartoons and movies as carrying a camera, being bucktoothed, and wearing glasses. It is true that the percentage of Japanese who wear glasses is

推計されていて、これは欧米人の約２倍に当たるとも言われています。

どうしてメガネ使用率が高いのかといえば、理由は単純で、日本人の半数以上が近視だからです。欧米人には遠視が多いのに対し、日本人や中国人には近視が多いとされています。ただこれは、「遺伝よりも生活習慣のほうに問題がある」という指摘もあります。子供の頃から勉強熱心で、読書量や仕事量が多いといった勤勉な姿勢が視力の低下を招いている部分はあるのでしょう。そのうえ、近年ではパソコンやTVゲームに向かう時間も長くなっているのですから、日本人の近視はますます増えていくかもしれません。

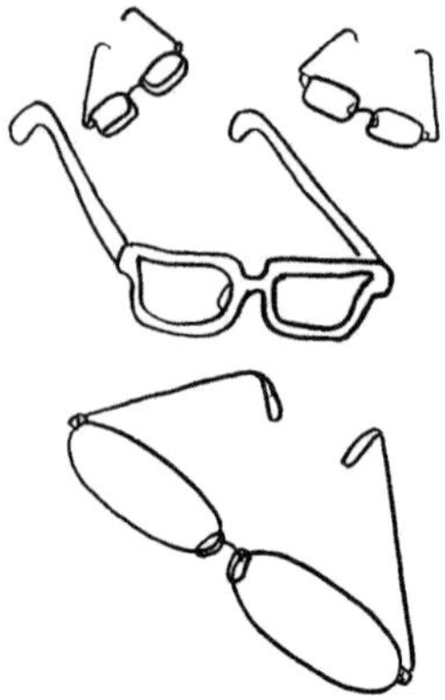

Qなぜ、花粉症の人がこんなに多いのですか？

欧米では「hay fever」とも言われるように干草が原因になることが多いようですが、日本の花粉症の多くはスギ花粉が原因となっています。1970年代中頃から花粉症患者が急増し、現在では全人口の20％が患者であるという統計もあり、大きな社会問題になっています。

戦後、家屋建築の需要を見込んで多くのスギが植林されましたが、その木が成長して、多くのスギ花粉を出すようになったのが原因と考えられます。

スギ林が多くある山村部よりは都市部に患者が多いというデータもあります。大気汚染との関係を指摘する声もある一方で、都市の方が花粉が飛散しやすい状況にあるからだという説もあり、まだ結論は出ていません。

high; it is thought to be somewhere between 30 and 40 percent. This is about twice that of Westerners.

Why should this be? The answer is simple. More than half of Japanese are shortsighted (or myopic). While farsightedness (also called hyperopia) seems to be common among Westerners, Japanese and Chinese are commonly nearsighted. Some say that this is not so much a matter of genetics as a matter of lifestyle. It may partly come from studying hard when a child, reading a lot, overusing the eyes in the workplace, and in general working long, hard hours. In recent years, children spend a lot of time watching TV and playing video games, and so shortsightedness may continue to increase into the future.

■ Why do so many Japanese get hay fever?

In English, this allergy is called hay fever because it was often caused by dried grass or hay. In Japan, it is most often caused by cedar pollen. In the mid 1970s the number of Japanese suffering from hay fever suddenly increased, and now it is said that 20 percent of the population suffers from hay fever, making it a serious health issue.

After the end of World War II, many cedar forests were planted in the expectation that the wood would be needed for building new homes. When these trees grew to maturity, they produced a good deal of pollen. This is thought to be the cause of the problem.

However, statistics indicate that there are more hay fever sufferers in cities than in mountainous areas. Some say that this shows the connection between hay fever and urban pollution, while others say that this merely shows that pollen spreads more easily in cities. As yet, there is no definitive answer.

なぜ、Q マスクをしている人がこんなに多いのですか？

欧米においてマスクといえば防塵マスク、手術マスクなどを指すように、日常生活の中でマスクをつける習慣がほとんどないため、日本で多くの人がマスクをつけているのを見ると、「SARS（重症急性呼吸器症候群）のような病気が流行しているのか⁉」と驚いてしまうようです。日本でも以前はこれほどマスク人口が多かったわけではありませんが、花粉症の流行とともに、次第に増えていったのです。最近は花粉の吸い込みを防ぐための立体型マスクなども開発されています

ただし、東南アジアでは、バイクに乗る人が粉塵などを吸わないようにマスクをすることが古くから習慣化していました。マスクをつけて人前に出ることへの抵抗感は、欧米人にくらべて小さいのは確かでしょう。アメリカでマスクをしていれば「銀行強盗と間違えられる」とのジョークもありますが、日本では、マスクをしているだけでそんな目で見られることはまずありません。

■ Why do so many Japanese wear face masks?

Since Westerners are not in the habit of wearing face masks (also called dust masks, surgical masks, and filter masks) as a part of their everyday lives, they are quite surprised when they come to Japan and see so many people wearing them. Sometimes you even hear a joke: "Has SARS or something broken out?" Japan did not always have such a large mask-wearing population, but the number of mask wearers gradually increased as hay fever became more common and masks that fit that shape of the face were developed to filter out pollen.

However, just as motorbike riders in Southeast Asia have long been in the habit of wearing masks to filter out dust, it is probably true that East Asians are less reluctant than Westerners to appear in public wearing masks. If you wear a face mask in the United States, you might be jokingly told, "You're going to be mistaken for a bank robber!" In Japan, of course, it would take something more than a face mask for that to happen.

6 性格

なぜ、Q 本音と建前を使い分けるのですか？

「日本人は本音と建前を使い分けるので、本心がわからない」とは、欧米人はもちろん、隣国である韓国や中国の人からもよく指摘される問題です。本音とは、その人がほんとうに考えていることであり、建前とは、立場上言わなければならないことをいいます。

自分の周囲で余計な軋轢を生み出さないようにするため、本心を隠すケースは、日本人にはたしかに多いのでしょう。余命の短い人に会ったとき、「顔色が悪いね」とは口にしないものですが、それが「本音と建前の使い分け」の本質といえます。その意味でいえば、世界中の人がそうした気遣いをしているはずですが、その「度合いの問題」として、日本人はそれが強いということでしょう。

これは、狭い島の中で、国を成してきた歴史とも関係しているのかもしれません。古代の政治家、聖徳太子（574-622）は、『十七条憲法』（604年）の中で「和をもって尊しとなす」と書いていますが、そうした姿勢は日本人の特性になっています。

本音を言い合ってお互いを傷つけるのは怖いし、ケンカをしても狭い島ですから、逃げるところもなく顔をつきあわせて暮らしていかなければなりません。そんなことだったら、本音を隠して、表面上は仲良くつきあっている方がいいという「生活の知恵」なのでしょう。

■ Why do Japanese make a distinction between what they think and what they say?

Americans and Europeans, as well as Chinese and Koreans, often say that it is hard to tell what Japanese really think because there is a gap between what they really think (*honne*) and what they say to meet social expectations (*tatemae*).

It cannot be denied that Japanese often hide their true feelings in order to avoid social conflict. For instance, if you visit someone who has a life-threatening illness, you don't mention the fact that they look a little pale. That is the essence of *honne* and *tatemae*. In that sense, people all over the world do the same thing. Maybe it is just a matter of degree, and Japanese tend to be at the higher end of the scale.

This phenomenon may be related to the history of this small, heavily populated island. Way back in the early seventh century, Prince Shōtoku (574-622) wrote a seventeen-article constitution, and the first article was "Value harmony and avoid conflict." This attitude has become characteristic of the Japanese mind.

Japanese are afraid to tell the truth and get into an argument, thus hurting people's feelings. And even if they should argue, there is no way to escape the results: they end up having to face the other person every day. To avoid this, it is better to hide one's true feelings and try to get along with people on the surface. I suppose this is one life lesson that Japanese have learned well.

なぜ、ほかの人と同じことをするのですか？

何かのブームが起きれば「右へ倣え」のようにそれに呼応するのは日本人だけではないはずですが、ファッションから行動まで他人と同じようにしがちな傾向はたしかに強いのかもしれません。

それはやはり、日本が島国であることと、歴史的に見ても、家制度、徒弟制度、終身雇用制度といった集団社会が形成されてきていた影響が強いと考えられます。そのため、個々の考えによって集団の足並みを乱すのは良くないという意識が根付いているわけです。

国際経営学者のロバート・マーチ氏は「箱の中の日本人」という言い方をしていますが、狭い社会の中で生きているため、人と同じことを好む性向や、本音と建前を使い分ける習慣、ノーと言わない姿勢が生まれてきた部分はあるのでしょう。

有名なジョークがあります。沈みかかった船で乗客が救命ボートに殺到したとき、女性や子供を先に乗せてください、と男性たちにたのんだときの船長の言葉です。彼はアメリカ人に向かっては「あなたは英雄になれますよ」と言いました。イギリス人に向かっては「あなたは紳士でしょう」。ドイツ人には「これは規則です」。そして日本人に向かっては「みなさんそうなさっていますよ」と言ったというのです。

なぜ、すぐに謝るのですか？

どんなときにでも簡単に謝るのは、争いを好まない性格のためなのでしょう。ただし、人に謝るということが、「自分の非を認めること」とイコールになるのだと認識できていない人が多すぎるのは問題です。交通事故の際などにも、どちらに非があったかを問わずに謝ってしまう人も少なくありませんが、そのことが自分の不利を招く場合もあるのだと知っておく必要はあるでしょう。

■ Why do Japanese always do what others are doing?

I don't suppose that Japanese are the only people who immediately fall into step with each new trend, but Japanese definitely have that tendency, whether it's the latest fashion in clothing or something else.

The importance of group thinking can be traced to the fact that Japan is an island country and to its group-oriented history, with its prewar family system, the old apprentice system, and the more recent lifelong employment system. As a result, it has become firmly ingrained in the Japanese mind that the individual should not disrupt group behavior.

The international economist Robert March once described Japanese as "living in a box," which seems appropriate. In any event, the experience of living in a tightly packed society has, to some extent, given rise to the tendency to do as others do, to the habit of paying particular attention to what one says (*honne* and *tatemae*), and to the inability to say "No."

There is a well-known joke about the Japanese mentality, which goes something like this. A ship is sinking, and everyone is trying to get into the lifeboats at the same time. The captain asks the four men to let the women and children go first. To the American, the captain says, "You'll be a hero." To the British, he says, "After all, you're a gentleman." To the German, he says, "It's the rule." And to the Japanese, he says, "It's what everyone else is doing."

■ Why are Japanese so eager to apologize?

The reason that Japanese are ready to apologize at the drop of a hat is that they want to avoid disagreements. Apologizing has become habitual, with no thought behind it. The problem is that there are too many people who don't realize that to apologize is to admit that they are wrong. When there has been a traffic accident, for example, a lot of people immediately apologize, even though it hasn't been determined yet who is at fault. Such people should realize that an immediate apology is not necessarily to their advantage.

なぜ、はっきり「ノー」と言わないのですか？

とにかく日本人は、人に対して「ノー」と言うことを嫌います。こう言うことによって相手の感情を害したくないという気持ちが強く働いているのです。そこで日本人は、断る可能性が高いケースにおいても「検討してみます」などと、言葉を濁す場合がよくあります。日本人同士であれば、その時点で「かなりノーに近い回答」と察せられ、検討してみるという言葉に相手の誠意を感じるものです。しかし、外国の人から見れば、その時点で答えが出ているのなら、なぜはっきり言ってくれないのだということになるわけです。

日本に長くいた留学生が国に帰って、親や友人から「おまえは賛成なのか反対なのか、はっきりしろ」と言われるケースがよくあるそうです。こういう気持ちは感染するものなのかもしれません。

なぜ、出身県によって性格が違うのですか？

出身県によって性格にある程度の傾向が見られるという意味で「県民性」という言葉がつくられました。かつての日本では、現在の47都道府県より細かい国や藩が形成されていました。その頃には交通も発達していなかったため、そうした国ごとの気候や文化、主要産業などの特徴によって、生活習慣の違いや地域的な気質というものが生まれてきたのだと考えられます。

たとえば、日本のほぼ中央に位置する愛知県は、織田信長、豊臣秀吉、徳川家康という三大武将の出身地で、そのためか、プライドが高く派手なことが大好きと言われています。

また、山口県は徳川幕府を倒す原動力となった土地だけに、議論好きで政治が大好き。日本の総理大臣の８人までがこの県の出身者です。

「京都の着倒れ、大阪の食い倒れ、江戸の買い倒れ」といった言葉もあります。これは、京都の人は着るものにお金を使い、大阪の人は食べ物にお金を使い、江戸（東

■ Why can't Japanese just say, "No"?

It's a fact—Japanese just don't like saying, "No." The underlying reason is that they want to avoid hurting people's feelings. Even when the answer is most likely to be in the negative, Japanese will still use expressions like "We'll look into it," and in that way avoid giving a straight answer. Between Japanese, it will be clear in this case that the answer is most likely "no"; by saying that they will look into it, the one party is showing consideration for the other party's feelings. But a foreigner would think it odd if he didn't get a clear answer even though a decision had already been made.

I have heard of cases in which foreign students go home after many years in Japan and are told by their parents and friends that they seem incapable of giving a straight answer anymore. This particular "sickness" is catching, it seems.

■ Why do different prefectures produce different personality types?

To a certain extent it is possible to guess someone's personality type by the prefecture they grew up in. A word was created specifically to express this idea—*kenmin-sei*, which we might loosely translate as "prefecture personality type." Japan now has 47 large administrative districts, of which 43 are prefectures. Before 1868 there were more regional divisions, and they were smaller, such as fiefs (*han*) and "countries" (*kuni*). Back then, it wasn't easy to travel long distances, and since each country had a somewhat different local climate, culture, and products, these differences produced further differences in lifestyles and personality types.

Take, for example, Aichi prefecture, which is located in central Japan. Aichi produced three of the greatest military leaders of Japanese history: Oda Nobunaga (1534-1582), Toyotomi Hideyoshi (1537-1598), and Tokugawa Ieyasu (1542-1616). Perhaps for that reason, the people of Aichi are said to have a lot of pride and to like doing things in a big way.

京）の人は遊興にお金を使うという傾向をあらわします。

出身地のなかでも、関東（東京都）と関西（大阪府）の人の性格は、とくによく比較されます。古くからの商業の町・大阪は「実利」を好み、新たに政治や文化の中心となった東京は、「見映え」を重視するといったようなものです。

なぜ、血液型を尋ねてくるのですか？

ふだん血液型などは気にしたこともない欧米の人たちは、日本人に血液型を尋ねられると、そんな質問をされたこと自体に驚きます。血液型による性格診断や相性占いは、科学的根拠に乏しいとされていますが、日本ではこれが広く親しまれています。

1916年に血液型と気質の関連に関する研究発表がなされて以来、血液型診断は何度かブームになっています。A型は神経質で、B型は自分勝手、O型は大ざっぱで、AB型は変人といったように、それこそ大ざっぱに分類していくものです。日本人の約40％はA型なので、かなりの割合で神経質タイプが該当する性格診断は、日本人にとっては「当たっている」ように感じられたのかもしれません。

On the other hand, Yamaguchi prefecture was at the center of the movement to bring down the Tokugawa shōgunate in the middle of the nineteenth century and form the new Meiji government. The people of Yamaguchi are said to love discussion and politics. Eight Japanese prime ministers have come from Yamaguchi.

There is a saying that points out the differences between people of Kyoto, Osaka, and Edo (the name of Tokyo before 1868). It is, "Kyotoites dress themselves into bankruptcy, Osakans eat themselves into bankruptcy, and Edoites play themselves into bankruptcy." This simply means that the people of Kyoto tend to spend a lot of money on clothing, those of Osaka on food, and those of Edo on personal entertainment.

Among the different regions and prefectures, the Kantō region (Tokyo) and the Kansai region (Osaka) are often brought up for comparison. An industrial center from olden times, Osaka emphasizes profit; as a new political and cultural center, Tokyo emphasizes appearance.

■ Why do Japanese ask what your blood type is?

Americans and Europeans usually don't give much thought to blood type, so they are somewhat surprised when Japanese ask about it. Even though there doesn't seem to be much of a scientific basis for judging character types or personality compatibility by means of blood types, Japanese are rather fond of doing so, anyway.

Following the publication of a report in 1916 on the relationship between blood type and character, crazes have occurred any number of times. Roughly, here is the character for each type. Type A worries about small things. B is self-centered. O is concerned with the big picture. AB is something of an oddball. Since about 40 percent of Japanese are A type, which would put them into the worrier category, many Japanese are quite satisfied with this categorization.

なぜ、日本人は無表情なのですか？

日本人はいつも表情を変えないので、何を考えているのかわからず怖いということは、以前から指摘されていました。身振り手振りをくわえながら、表情豊かに会話するアメリカ人などにくらべれば、日本人の感情表現が乏しいのは確かでしょう。

日本の古い言葉に「男は三年に片頬」というものがあります。これは、男であれば片頬だけを動かしてかすかに笑うことが３年に１回程度あればいい、ということを言っているものです。もちろん、これは極端な言い回しですが、男は人前で自分の感情を表すものではないという考えが一般的だったのです。女性にしても、笑うときには手で口をかくすのがマナーになっていました。

現在、こうした考え方はなくなり、好感をもたれるためには表情が豊かな方がいいとは分かっているのですが、何百年と動かさなかった筋肉をときほぐすのに時間がかかっていると言うことなのです。

なぜ、すぐに年齢を尋ねてくるのですか？

企業などの集団社会において、年齢や勤続年数を尊重して地位や賃金を決めるシステムを「年功序列」といいます。そうしたシステム上の問題に限らず、一般社会においても、自分より年長の人に対しては敬意を表すべきだという考えが日本では徹底しています。儒教の影響も大きいのでしょう。

年長者に対しては、名前に「さん」を付けて呼び、年下に対しては「くん」を付けて呼ぶのが一般的です。また、年長者には敬語を用いるのがマナーなので、相手の年齢がわからなければどういう態度をとるべきかが定まらず、気分的にも落ち着きません。

そのため、すぐに年齢を尋ねてしまうのですが、自分が年長者とわかった段階で、すぐに「さん」を「くん」に変えたりするのは失礼とされています。

■ Why do so many Japanese have poker faces?

For some time now, Japanese have been described as having poker faces, and since it's hard to tell what they are thinking, they're a little scary. Compared with an American, say, who talks with a lot of facial expression and bodily gestures, I suppose it's true that Japanese don't show their emotions that much.

There is an old saying that goes something like, "For a man, a half a laugh every three years is enough." Literally, it says that if a man laughs with just one cheek every three years, that is enough. This is taking things to an extreme, I admit, but in the past it was generally agreed that a man shouldn't show his emotions in public. For a woman, etiquette called for her to cover her mouth when laughing.

Now, of course, things have changed, and we realize that if you want to make a good impression, the livelier your expression, the better. Still, facial muscles that have been out of use for hundreds of years cannot be brought back to life just like that.

■ Why do Japanese ask immediately how old you are?

In companies and organizations that are group oriented, one's position and salary are based on age and years of service. This is the so-called seniority system. Aside from the importance of one's age in this system, the thinking that older people deserve to be shown respect is widespread throughout Japanese society. This is due, in large part, to the influence of Confucianism.

It is common practice to put "-san" after someone's name who is older than you, and "-kun" after the name of someone who is younger. It is also considered proper manners to use "polite language"—that is, respectful language—when speaking to someone older. But if you don't know the age of the person you are talking to, you can't tell what level of politeness to adopt, and you end up feeling frustrated and uneasy.

Of course, it is considered impolite to suddenly stop referring to the other person as "-san" and immediately adopt "-kun" because you have realized that you are the older of the two.

なぜ、Q 日本人はこんなにカメラが好きなのですか？

日本製のカメラが世界中に出回ったということもあるかもしれません。日本人がカメラ好きだというイメージは世界的に定着しているようです。日本の世帯の70％以上には最低１台のカメラがあるとの調査結果も出ていますが、最近の携帯電話にはほとんどカメラ機能がついていることを考えれば、100％近いとも言えそうです。

最近のデジタルカメラの普及でフィルムの現像、焼付けが不要になったことで、カメラは生活の必需品に近いものになってきました。とくにブログが流行している現在は、「写真付きの日記」を公開する人が増えているので、レストランなどで自分が頼んだ食事を撮影している姿までが見かけられるようになっています。

こうした背景には、収集癖にも近い「記録欲」があるのではないかと考えられます。つまり、その場で感動するだけでは満足できず、その感動を「形あるもの」として手元に残しておきたいという欲求が強いのです。日本人には、一度しか読まない本でも図書館を利用せずに書店で購入し、本棚に並べておかないと気が済まない人が多いのですが、それと同じ発想なのでしょう。

カメラ機能付き携帯電話やブログ、デジタルカメラの普及によって、日本人のカメラ好きは、歯止めがきかなくなっていくのかもしれません。

なぜ、Q 温泉が好きなのですか？

世界の活火山の約10％がある火山国・日本には約２万の温泉があるとされ、複数の施設が集まった「温泉地」の数は3000を超えます。しかも、温泉はケガや病気に効能があるとされているのですから、風呂好きの日本人が積極的にそれを利用するのも当然でしょう。

17世紀頃から温泉に入って療養する「湯治」の習慣

■ Why do Japanese like cameras so much?

The Japanese fondness for cameras may have something to do with the fact that Japanese-made cameras have penetrated almost every corner of the globe. Almost wherever you go, the impression that Japanese love cameras seems firmly established. One survey indicates that over 70 percent of Japanese households have at least one camera. And given the fact that almost all recently made cell phones have a built-in camera, I would say that the number is close to 100 percent.

Since digital cameras don't need to have film exposed or photos printed, they have become more and more a part of everyday life. In particular, with the popularity of blogs, more and more people are uploading photo diaries, and you even see people taking pictures of the food they have just ordered at a restaurant.

It makes one think that, just as there are people who are crazy about collecting certain objects, there are also people who have an extraordinary desire to record what they have just experienced. Such people are not satisfied with the thrill of the moment; they are moved to transform that moment into something physical that they can keep close at hand. The thinking here may be similar to that of people who insist on buying books that they will read only once and lining them up on a shelf instead of borrowing them from the library. There are a lot of people like that in Japan.

What with cell phones that double as cameras, blogs, and the widespread use of digital cameras, there seems to be no end to the Japanese love affair with cameras.

■ Why do Japanese like hot springs so much?

Ten percent of the world's active volcanos are located in Japan. Japan has about 20,000 hot springs, and there are over 3,000 hot springs complexes with multiple facilities. Further, since hot springs are said to be good for injuries and various illnesses, it makes sense that Japanese, who like hot baths anyway, should be eager to make use of such facilities.

が一般にも根付いていきました。そして、多くの温泉地には宿泊施設、遊興施設が形成されていき、湯治のほかに、観光旅行、新婚旅行などに利用されるようになっていたのです。

これまでは温泉がなかった場所でも、お金をかけて深くまで掘り下げ源泉開発をすれば、かなりの確率で温泉を掘り当てられることがわかり、交通の便のいい場所に「日帰り入浴施設」をつくるのがブームとなっています。

各家庭にお風呂が普及したことで一般的な銭湯は減少していますが、ジャグジーや露天風呂といったレジャー的な付加価値を付けた「スーパー銭湯」は飛躍的に増えています。

Q なぜ、ボジョレー・ヌーヴォーが好きなのですか？

フランスのボジョレーで生産され、毎年11月第3木曜日の午前0時に販売が解禁される赤ワイン、ボジョレー・ヌーヴォーの消費量では、日本がフランスに次ぐ世界第2位になっています。

バブル時代の1980年代に仕掛けられた広告戦略がブームの始まりとされていますが、日本人はこうした「初物」や「カウントダウン的イベント」に乗せられやすい性質を持っているようです。日付変更線の関係で、世界で最初に解禁日を迎えられるという特権意識がブームの発端でした。日付が変わると同時にコルクを開けるカウントダウン・パーティーも珍しくありません。

バブル崩壊によって一時はブームもすたれましたが、1990年代後半から赤ワインブームが起きたため、現在では、解禁日にボジョレー・ヌーヴォーを飲むことが定着しています。

Since the seventeenth century, the healing powers of hot springs has been commonly accepted. Since then, most hot spring resorts have built accommodations for staying overnight and have added amusement facilities. Thus, in addition to their attraction as a means of therapy, hot springs came to be a favorite spot for tourists and newlyweds.

Even in localities where there are no natural hot springs, it is now known that if you can afford to dig deep enough, you can find the source of a hot spring with relatively ease. As a result, there is now a surge of activity in creating conveniently located day-trip hot springs.

With the spread of ordinary baths to the individual home, the traditional public bath has gone into decline. On the other hand, the building of "super hot springs" with jacuzzis, open-air baths, and other leisure add-ons has skyrocketed.

■ Why do Japanese like Beaujolais nouveau?

Beaujolais nouveau is a red wine produced in the Beaujolais region of France and officially goes on sale at midnight every year on the third Thursday of November. It enjoys greater sales in Japan than any other country except France. Its popularity has its origins in an ad campaign during the 1980's economic bubble, but Japanese are, in any event, easy prey for anything that is the first of the season or for a countdown to anything. Because of the International Date Line, Japan is the first country in which the wine is released. This feeling of somehow having an advantage was the spark that set off the boom. As the moment of the official release approaches, it is not unusual to have countdown parties at which corks are popped as the day changes.

With the collapse of the economic bubble, the craze for Beaujolais nouveau declined. But then, at the end of the 1990s, red wine again became a fad, and now drinking Beaujolais nouveau on release day is an established custom.

Qなぜ、こんなに貯金が好きなのですか？

日本では福祉に関する整備が遅れていました。戦後30年近くも経った1973年が「福祉元年」と呼ばれていることでもわかりますが、公的年金制度や医療保険制度などは、なかなか整えられないままでいました。そのため、貯金は老後の生活費、あるいは不測の事態に備えた貯えだったのです。

元来、日本人は危機回避志向が強い国民とも言われています。そうした性格が、儒教の影響でもある「倹約精神」と結びつき、稼いだお金をすぐに使い切るのではなく、「大切に使って、残りは貯金するのが美徳」という考え方が広まっていきました。

また、同じ危機回避志向から、株式や投資信託などリスクのある資産運用をしようとはしませんでした。消費欲がもっとも高まっていたと言われる高度経済成長期においても貯蓄率は飛躍的に伸びていたのですから、日本人の堅実性がよくわかります。

長い不況が続いていた日本ですが、現在でも貯金総額は1400兆円を超えると言われています。この貯金を消費に回せばすぐに景気は回復すると指摘されていましたが、不況という社会不安があるからこそ、貯金が大切だと考える人は多かったわけです。

Qなぜ、最近、株を買う人が増えたのですか？

最大の要因としては、デイトレードが身近になったことが挙げられます。かつての株式売買は手数料が高かったため、１日のうちに頻繁に売買を繰り返すデイトレードは一般的ではありませんでした。しかし、1999年に手数料が完全自由化されたあとには、即時性が高いデイトレードが個人投資家の注目を浴びるようになったのです。

さらに、パソコンやインターネットの飛躍的な普及

■ Why do Japanese like to save?

Social welfare in Japan got off to a late start. This can be seen from the fact that the year 1973, almost thirty years after the end of the war, is known as the first year of the welfare age. The national pension plan, health insurance, and much more remained in very poor shape. Accordingly, personal savings were seen as an important means of support in old age and as protection against an unpredictable future.

It seems to be part of the basic nature of the Japanese people to avoid trouble by taking preventive measures. When this tendency is combined with the Confucian virtue of being careful with your money, the attitude takes hold that money earned should not be used up immediately, but should be used exceedingly carefully, and what is left over should be saved.

This same attitude prevented people from investing in risky undertakings like stocks and funds. Even during the high-growth period around the 1960s when consumer spending was strong, savings grew dramatically. From this alone, you can see how practical the Japanese are.

During the recent economic slowdown, total savings amounted to more than ¥1,400 trillion. If this money had been used for consumption, the economy would have improved immediately. But since many people still feared bad economic times, they clung to the idea that saving was important.

■ Why are so many more people investing in stocks?

The biggest factor is that day trading has become so much easier. In the past the commission for trading stock was high, so that day trading, which involves repeated trades in a single day, was not common. However, after commission fees were liberalized in 1999, individual investors were attracted by the immediate results of day trading.

Furthermore, due to the dramatic spread of the personal computer and the Internet, as well as the maturing of security firms' online services, the buying and selling of stock became much more user-

と、証券会社のオンラインサービスの充実によって、株の売買が、より手軽なものになりました。そのため、家庭の主婦なども、ゲーム感覚やお小遣い稼ぎ感覚で株式売買を行えるようになったのです。

そんな中、デイトレードで巨額の利益を得たカリスマ投資家が出現したり、株式の操作によって巨万の富を得た企業などが出現したりしたことで、株式売買はさらに注目を集めるようになりました。ただし、誰もが利益を出せるわけではないのは自明の理なので、市場の状況次第では、一気に熱が冷める可能性もないわけではありません。

friendly. This resulted in housewives and others taking up trading in stock as if it were a video game or a simple means of earning some pocket money.

Meanwhile, a few charismatic investors raked in huge profits through day trading, and corporations became unbelievably rich by manipulating stock prices. All of this brought more attention to the stock market. But, of course, it goes without saying that not everyone is going to make a profit. Depending on what happens now, the sudden interest in trading could just as quickly fade away.

7 社会

Qなぜ、

日本は治安がいいのですか？

2005年度版の『犯罪白書』によれば、2004年の犯罪件数は343万件で、このうち道路上の交通事故に係るものを除けば256万件になるとされています。近年、日本の犯罪件数は増加傾向にあり、2002年には戦後最多を記録しました。

その後は横ばい傾向（やや減少傾向）になっていますが、かつてのように「治安の良さ」を誇りにできなくなっています。凶悪犯罪が増加しているうえ、刑法犯検挙率も落ちているので、かつてのような安心感はなくなりつつあるのが事実です。それでも、アメリカと犯罪発生率をくらべれば、殺人で約５分の１、強姦で約18分の１、強盗で約35分の１となります。

日本の治安がいい理由のひとつとして「交番」制度があげられます。これは、町の各所に警察官ひとりかふたりのミニ警察署をおくもので、海外でもKOBANとして知られるようになりました。

Qなぜ、

女性がもっと活躍しないのですか？

古代には女性天皇もいたように、女性の地位は低いものではありませんでした。それが中世の武士社会の発達とともに男尊女卑の風潮が広まったと言われています。また明治時代（1868-1912）には、戸主に家の統率権限を与える「家制度」がつくられたので、女性には戸主への従属的な役割が当てはめられました。

工業化が進んだ大正時代（1912-1926）には「男は仕事、女は家庭」という役割分担が一般化していき、戦後

Society?

■ Why is Japan's crime rate so low?

According to the 2005 White Paper on Crime issued by the Japanese government, the number of crimes in 2004 was 3,430,000. If the number of traffic accidents is subtracted, the total is 2,560,000. Overall, the number of crimes in Japan has recently been increasing, with 2002 having the highest number in the postwar period.

Since 2002, crime has leveled out or slightly declined, but in any case Japan can no longer proudly point to its low crime rate. While the number of violent crimes has increased, the rate of criminal arrests has gone down. The sense of safety that Japanese once enjoyed has, without a doubt, suffered. Still, as far as the crime rate is concerned, Japan's homicide rate is about one-fifth that of the United States, rape one-eighteenth, and robbery one thirty-fifth.

One reason given for Japan's comparative low crime rate is the system of placing small police stations with one or two officers at appropriate places around town. This *kōban* system has attracted quite a bit of attention abroad.

■ Why aren't Japanese women more active in public life?

In ancient times, the position of Japanese women in society was not particularly low, as can be seen from the fact that the emperor's throne was occupied by a woman on a number of occasions. However, apparently due to the rise to power of the samurai class, the role of women in the medieval period became decidedly secondary. In the Meiji period (1868-1912), the household system made the husband the head of the household, and the wife's interests were subjugated to his.

の高度経済成長期にはその傾向がいっそう強まりました。これは、この頃の日本では核家族が増えていたため、夫婦のうちどちらかが育児や家事を行わなければならなかったことと、この頃には第２次産業が中心だったため、ブルーカラーの労働層が求められていたことが関係しています。

1980年代から脱工業化社会に向かいだしたため、女性の社会進出は少しずつ増えていきました。1986年には「男女雇用機会均等法」が施行され、女性雇用の状況も改善に向かいはじめました。

この法ではまだ、男女の均等処遇は事業主の努力義務に過ぎなかったのですが、1999年の改正によって、女性への不利益な差別が禁じられました。このように日本社会の構図は大きく変わりだし、企業のトップに立つ女性の数も、これまでにくらべてはっきりと増えています。

2005年に国連開発計画（ＵＮＤＰ）は、国別に見た「女性の働きやすさ」をランキングで指標化しましたが、それによれば日本は80ヵ国中43位でした。「文明国」への道はまだ遠いようです。

なぜ、名前よりも姓を先に言うのですか？

日本人の名前は、古くから一貫して「名字（姓）→名前」の順序であらわされてきました。親しい関係でなければ、名前では呼び合わず、名字に「さん」を付けて呼ぶのが一般的です。「さん」は英語のMr.やMrs.のようなもので、相手が男でも女でも使うことができます。

ただし、名前をローマ字表記する際には「名前→名

With the growth of industrialization in the Taishō period (1912-1926), it became commonly accepted that the man's place was at work, the woman's place at home. This pattern became even more pronounced in the postwar period of rapid economic development during the late 1950s, 1960s, and early 1970s. As the number of nuclear families increased, it was felt that one of the parents should stay at home to do the housework and take care of the children. An additional factor may have been that since the secondary sector of industry (manufacturing and construction) was at the center of economic growth during this period, this family arrangement was the one favored by the blue collar workers engaged in this sector.

From the 1980s onward, with the movement toward a postindustrial society, women began to play a greater role in society. In 1986 the Law for Equal Employment Opportunity of Men and Women was enacted, and employment conditions began to show some improvement.

However, the responsibility for seeing that equal treatment was carried out was left to the employer, and it was only with the revision of the law in 1999 that unfair discrimination against women was effectively made illegal. With this, Japanese society began to show some substantial changes, and the number of women now occupying top managerial positions is much greater than ever before.

Still, when the United Nations Development Programme (UNDP) looked at women's working conditions for 2005, its indicator ranked Japan as forty-third among eighty countries. It appears that there is still a lot of work to be done.

■ Why is the family name given before the personal name?

From olden times, Japanese have given their family name first, followed by their personal (or given) name. And unless you are on close terms with someone, you shouldn't call them by their given name but rather by their family name followed by a suffix like -san (-san is used somewhat like "Mr." and "Mrs." except that it doesn't indicate gender).

字」の順に変えるのが慣習になっていました。これは、明治時代に欧米のルールに合わせようとしたためですが、現在はこの慣習についても見直されてきています。英語の教科書も「名字→名前」方式を採用しています。中国人や韓国人の名前も「名字→名前」の順であらわされますが、ローマ字表記をしてもその順序を変えていないので、日本だけ他国のルールに合わせて名前を呼び変える必要はないと考えたからです。

とはいっても、韓国は名字の数が500、中国では300くらいと少ないうえ、漢字で書けば、ほとんど1文字なので、名字か名前かというのはすぐ分かります。ところが日本の名字は30万くらいあるうえに、ほとんどが2文字で名前とまぎらわしく、また1文字から3文字、4文字のもあって複雑です。

外国人との仕事が多い人は、名字は大文字で、名前は小文字で書くような工夫をしています。

Qなぜ、こんなに狭い都道府県に分かれているのですか？

約37万8000 km^2という面積しかない日本に47の都道府県があるのですから、分割しすぎだとは言えるのかもしれません。しかし、アメリカの州のように独立性は高くないので、そんなに不都合はありません。

こうした都道府県分けは、歴史とも大きく関係していて、古代、大和朝廷の支配下には30前後の国があったと考えられています。その後はさらに60余国に細分化されていき、江戸時代には約300の藩がそれぞれの国を持っていました。それが明治維新後の1871年に藩を廃して、北海道のほか3府72県ができました。そして、その後の再編によって現在の47都道府県（東京都、北

Not too long ago, Japanese commonly gave their personal name first and their family name last when writing their name in the Latin (or Roman) alphabet. This custom started in the Meiji period (1868-1912) when Japanese were trying hard to fit in with American and European ways of doing things. Recently, however, this practice is being reconsidered. In English textbooks published in Japan, for example, when Japanese names are listed in the Latin alphabet, they are given with the family name first. Since Chinese and Koreans also place their family name first, and they make no attempt to change that order when using the Latin alphabet, some feel that there is no reason for Japanese to do it, either.

And yet, Korea has only about 500 family names, and Chinese only about 300. Most of them, when written in Chinese characters, are written with one character, and it is easy to tell which is the family name and which the personal name. In the case of Japan, the situation is a little more complicated. There are around 300,000 family names written with one to four Chinese characters, though most consist of two.

Some Japanese who work with foreigners a lot use the Japanese order but make an effort to avoid confusion by printing their family name in capital letters and their personal name in smaller letters.

■ Why are there so many large administrative districts?

Since the area of Japan covers only about 378,000 square kilometers (145,883 square miles), it could be said that Japan is divided up into too many large administrative divisions—47 in all. On the other hand, however, since these divisions don't have the administrative independence of US states, there is little chance for conflict with the central government in Tokyo.

These large administrative divisions have their roots in Japanese history. During the Yamato period (approximately 300-710) there is said to have been about thirty "countries" under the imperial court's control. Later this number grew to over sixty, and in the Edo period (1600-1868) there were approximately 300 fiefs (or *han*), each with

海道、大阪府、京都府と43の県）ができたのです。もともと異なる統治下に置かれていた地域をまとめようとすれば難しい問題も出てくるものなので、近代においてはこのかたちが妥当だったと言えるでしょう。

ただ、終戦後まもない頃から行政区域をさらにまとめる「道州制」が検討されていて、現在も議論は続けられています。道州制では9、11、13に分割する案が出ています。

Qなぜ、憲法を変えようとしているのですか？

第２次世界大戦で連合国に降伏した日本は、軍国主義の排除や徹底的民主化などが義務付けられたポツダム宣言を受諾しました。そのため終戦後には、日本を占領していた連合国総司令部（ＧＨＱ）から「憲法改正」の勧告を受けました。

そこで日本政府は改正案を作成しましたが、旧来の大日本帝国憲法（1889年に制定された明治憲法）から脱却しきれていない内容だったため、連合国最高司令官のマッカーサーに却下されています。そして結局は、ＧＨＱ側が作成した試案、いわゆる「ＧＨＱ草案」をもとにして現行憲法が制定されたのです。

現行憲法は、三大基本原理として、「基本的人権の尊重」、「国民主権（主権在民）」、「平和主義（戦争の放棄）」を挙げています。この三大基本原理のうち、平和主義の解釈については、独立国家としての自衛権までを放棄することを意味するのかどうかと長年にわたって議論されてきました。

また制定過程にＧＨＱが関与していたことから「押し

its own ruling lord. In 1871, when the industrialization and modernization of Japan began, the fiefs were abolished, and in their place were established, aside from Hokkaido, three metropolitan areas (*fu*) and seventy-two prefectures (*ken*). Still later, a further reorganization resulted in forty-seven large administrative units—one "metropolis" (*to*; Tokyo), one "circuit" (*dō*; Hokkaido), two "urban prefectures" (*fu*; Osaka and Kyoto), and forty-three prefectures (*ken*). Although trying to integrate administrative areas that were formerly under different ruling powers could not have been easy, the present arrangement seems about right.

However, soon after the end of World War II, discussions began about further reducing the number of administrative divisions. These discussions are still going on, and proposals have been made for creating nine, eleven, or thirteen large administrative divisions.

■ Why is there a movement to revise the constitution?

At the end of World War II, Japan accepted the Potsdam Declaration and surrendered to the Allied Powers. The Potsdam Declaration called for, among other things, the abolishment of the Japanese army and the complete democratization of Japan. With the occupation of Japan, the Supreme Commander of the Allied Powers (SCAP; usually referred to as GHQ in Japan) ordered a revision of the Japanese constitution.

When the Japanese government presented its recommendations for revision, they were not that different from the older Meiji Constitution, which had been enacted in 1889. These recommendations were rejected by Supreme Commander General Douglas MacArthur. In the end, a draft drawn up by MacArthur's staff became the basis for the present constitution.

The current constitution has three main principles: respect for fundamental human rights; the sovereignty of the people (that is, the people are the ultimate source of political power, not the emperor); and the renunciation of war (that is, the nation gives up its right to wage war). Of these three, the third one has long been a subject of

つけられた憲法」だという批判的な声も絶えません。最近再び、憲法改正をめぐる議論が活発化しています。

Qなぜ、ノートにプラスチックの板を挟んでいるのですか？

欧米では使用する習慣がないようですが、「下敷き」という文房具です。日本では、小学生の頃から、ノートに記入する際には紙と紙のあいだに下敷きを挟むように指導されます。下敷きを使うと、ノートに文字を記入していても、次のページに跡が残らないようになります。画数の多い漢字を書く際には、アルファベットを書くときよりも指先に力が込められやすいとも考えられます。また、日本の小学校では、ＨＢの鉛筆を使って力強く文字を書くように指導するのが一般的なので、余計に跡が残りやすくなるのでしょう。

ただし、中学、高校と進むにつれて鉛筆を使うこともなくなり、下敷きも使われなくなります。

Qなぜ、若い人は読書しなくなったのですか？

日本人には本好きが多いという印象があるのかもしれませんが、近年では「活字離れ」が問題視されています。ひと月に1冊も本を読まない無読率は50％前後を推移していると見られ、1980年代には10％程度だった大学生の無読率も、最近は40％近い数字になっているという調査結果も出ています。

そうした中にあって、難解な純文学などは敬遠され、わかりやすさとエンターテインメント性のほうが重要視

debate concerning whether it means that the nation has given up its fundamental right to self-defense.

Further, since the GHQ was involved in its forming, the constitution has long been viewed by some as having been "forced" upon Japan. Recently, the debate over revising the constitution has once again become quite lively.

■ Why do Japanese students use a plastic sheet in their notebooks?

What we are referring to here is, of course, the stationary item that Japanese call a *shitajiki*, but which is apparently not used in the United States or Europe, and has no name in English. In Japanese elementary schools, children are taught to put a sheet of plastic under the page they are writing on in their notebooks. By using the *shitajiki*, no marks or impressions appear on the following page. It is possible that the sheet is needed because more pressure is used when writing complex kanji than when writing the alphabet. Further, elementary school children are generally taught to use HB pencils and to write with a firm hand, which means that an impression is likely to be created on the following page.

However, as students move on to junior and senior high school, pencils are no longer used, meaning that the *shitajiki* are no longer needed.

■ Why is it that young people don't read much anymore?

Generally speaking, Japanese have long been known as book lovers, but recently there has been a troubling movement away from reading. Apparently the percentage of people who don't read a single book per month has moved up to around 50 percent, and according to one survey, the percentage of non-reading university students, which was 10 percent in the 1980s, has recently moved close to 40 percent.

There is no doubt that serious literature is now avoided, and ease

されているのは確かでしょう。近年では、小説とアニメ風のイラストを一体化した「ライトノベル」と呼ばれるジャンルが生まれ、急成長しています。また、高視聴率をあげた恋愛ドラマを平易な文章でノベライズしてベストセラーになるケースも多いように、小説に対しても、マンガを読んだりドラマや映画を観たりするのに近いお手軽さを求める人が増えているのです。
　単に活字離れという問題として捉えるのではなく、「知的水準の低下」の問題として取り上げるべきだという指摘の声も出ています。

なぜQ 日本のブログには、日記的なものが多いのですか？

　誰もが簡単にインターネットで発信できるように作られた「ブログ」というツールが、世界的な広がりを見せています。ただし、欧米諸国では、主に議論や情報発信に用いられるのに対して、日本では個人的な日記を書くのに利用されるケースが多いようです。
　こうした違いが出てきた理由のひとつにはブログが広がった経緯があるのでしょう。アメリカでブログが浸透しはじめたのは、2001年の「9・11」、いわゆる「同時多発テロ」を契機にしていると言われています。安否が確認できない家族を探すためや、自分がわかる範囲の身近な情報を発信するためでした。
　アメリカではこのような非常時における発信からブログが普及していったため、メディアツールとしての認識が高くなっています。このため、今でも議論や情報発信に用いられるケースが多いものと考えられます。
　一方、日本では、ブログの普及に「タレントブログ」の存在が大きな影響を与えています。つまり、著名人がブログで日記を書くことによって、ブログの存在を知らしめていったのです。このため、どうしても「ブログ＝日記」という認識が強くなったというわけです。
　また、ひとりあたりのブログの利用時間がもっとも長

of reading and entertainment value have assumed a more important role. A recent development has been the rapid growth in what are known as "light novels," which are a combination of anime-like illustrations with fiction. Furthermore, there seems to be a definite increase in the number of people who want to read something that is as easy on the brain as a manga or a TV drama or a movie. This trend is seen in the great number of bestsellers produced in the form of simply written novelizations of highly-rated romantic television dramas.

Some feel that this shows not only a movement away from books, but an actual drop in intelligence level.

■ Why are Japanese blogs mostly diaries?

The blog, a tool that makes it easy for almost anyone to publish their thoughts on the Internet, is becoming worldwide in scope. In Europe and the United States, blogs are used mainly for discussion and the spread of information, while in Japan they are mostly used for writing personal diaries.

One reason for this difference lies in how blogs first came to be widely used in different countries. In the United States, it is said the event that caused blogs to become more widely known was 9/11, the terrorist attacks on the World Trade Center. In order to search for family whose safety could not be confirmed, people uploaded whatever information they had into blogs.

Because the blog was widely used in a time of crisis as a means of making information available, Americans became highly aware of it as a media tool. For that reason, the blog is still most often used for information and discussion.

In Japan, on the other hand, the blog was popularized by so-called celebrity blogs. Thanks to celebrities and other well-known people writing personal diaries, the existence of the blog became known to a wider audience, and the "blog equals diary" connection followed as a matter of course.

Incidentally, the country that records the most blog time per per-

いのはフランスです。フランスは伝統的にカフェで論争する文化があり、それをブログ上でやるから、というのがその理由です。

ブログにはそれぞれの国民性が出るようです。

なぜQ アパートや銭湯で外国人を差別するのですか？

「外国人だから」という理由だけで一様に差別をする風潮はあまりないはずですが、アパートの賃貸や入浴施設への入場をめぐってのトラブルはあります。それでも、アパートなどの賃貸住宅を借りにくいということについては、外国人だけの問題とはいえません。日本人であっても、保証人がいなかったり、定期的な収入が認められなければ、なかなか契約を結べないようになっています。夜間の出入りが多くて、転職する比率が高い水商売の女性の契約は、一律に認めない物件などもあるほどです。

外国人に関していえば、「入居者１人」という契約を結んでいながら、10人近い人たちが同居しているケースもあるそうです。また、日本ではゴミの出し方などについても細かいルールがあるので、言葉の問題も含めて、そうしたルールを理解してもらえるかどうかという不安もあります。このようなことから外国人を拒否する大家もいるのです。とはいえ、一部の外国人の行為を理由に、「外国人だから」という理由だけですべての外国人に対して賃貸を拒否するのは不当です。

同じような問題が入浴施設でも起こりました。入浴施設には「体を洗ってから入浴する」「湯船にタオルをつけない」「湯船で体や頭を洗わない」といったマナーがありますが、これを破った外国人がいたことからすべての外国人をしめだし、裁判になったケースがあったのです。

日本が世界に対して「開かれた」社会を作っていくためにも、改善しなければならないポイントの１つでしょう。

son is France. The French have a tradition of discussing things at cafes, and now they seem to be doing it via blogs.

Even with blogs, each country seems to have its own way of doing things.

■ Why are foreigners discriminated against when renting an apartment or using the public bath?

While I don't believe Japanese generally discriminate against foreigners just because they are foreigners, it is true that there have recently been some disturbing cases involving the renting of apartments to foreigners and their use of public baths. However, it should be pointed out that the difficulties of renting are not exclusively confined to foreigners. Even for Japanese, it is difficult to finalize a contract if the prospective renter does not have a guarantor or is without a regular income. Some rentals automatically exclude people who are likely to go in and out at odd hours of the night and women who have unstable jobs like bar hostesses.

Concerning foreigners, there seems to have been cases where the contract called for one occupant, but in fact there were nearly ten. Furthermore, there is the matter of how to put out the garbage properly, about which Japan has some rather detailed rules. Given the language problems involved, some worry that these rules won't be properly understood. As a result of issues like these, there are some Japanese landlords who reject foreigners out of hand. It seems unreasonable, however, to refuse to rent to all foreigners because of the behavior of a few.

There were similar problems regarding public baths. Public baths have many rules, such as 1) wash before getting into the tub, 2) don't take your towel with you into the bath, 3) don't wash your body or hair while in the tub, etc. There was one instance where some foreigners didn't follow the rules, so all foreigners were refused entry from then on. This case ended up in court.

This is one area that must be improved upon if Japan is going to be recognized as an "open society" by the rest of the world.

なぜ、クリスマス・イブがデートの日なのですか？

日本で行事としてのクリスマスが始まったのは1900年頃といわれています。その後、子供雑誌などで紹介されて、1920年代にはクリスマス・ケーキも登場し、プレゼントを交換する習慣が定着しました。

それでも、家族が揃ってケーキを食べていたうちは、欧米のクリスマスと過ごし方は似ていたと言えるはずです。しかし、1970年代後半からは、若い男女はカップルでクリスマス・イブを過ごすという風潮が強くなっていきました。

バブル時代の1980年代には、クリスマス・イブが若い男女にとっての最大のイベントのようにも位置づけられて、女性をいかに満足させられるかによって男性のステータスが問われるようにもなってしまいました。そのため、クリスマス・イブには高級レストランや高級ホテルを予約することもままならないようになったほどです。

このように日本のクリスマスはキリスト教とはほとんど関係なく、商業戦略あるいはメディア戦略に先導された「年末のイベント」となっているのです。

■ Why is Christmas Eve a big day for dating?

It is said that Christmas Eve first became an event of some importance in Japan around 1900. Thereafter it was introduced in children's magazines and other publications; the "Christmas cake" made its appearance in the 1920s; and the practice of exchanging gifts gradually became a custom.

All in all, eating Christmas cake surrounded by one's family should be no different in Japan than it is in the United States and Europe. Since the end of the 1970s, however, the custom of young people spending Christmas Eve together has gathered strength.

During the bubble economy of the 1980s, Christmas Eve rose to the position of being one of the most important events for young couples, and young men were judged by how well they could satisfy the desires of their dates on that day. As a result, it became extremely difficult to make reservations at top-notch restaurants and first-class hotels.

Thus, Christmas in Japan has almost nothing to do with Christianity, but has become another year-end event under the strategic guidance of commercial influences and media coverage.

8 世代

Q なぜ、若い人たちの髪は茶色いのですか？

日本人の髪の色はもともと黒いのですが、1990年代以降、髪を茶色に染めることが流行しています。髪型やファッションなどには時代ごとのブームがありますが、髪の毛を染めるのがこれほど流行ったことは、考えてみれば世界的にも珍しい現象でしょう。

80年代まで、髪を染めることは「特殊なファッション」と見られていましたが、90年代初頭から少しずつ「一般的なファッション」になっていき、90年代中頃からは、かなりの割合の若者が髪を染めるようになりました。

とくに、男性もこれに従ったのが今回の流行の最大の特徴です。茶色い髪を略して「茶髪（チャパツ）」と呼ぶことも一般化して、90年代後半には中年層でも茶髪にしている人が珍しくなくなりました。

「黒い髪は重い感じがしてやぼったいのに対して、茶髪は軽い感じがする」などとも説明されていましたが、その背景には西洋人の容姿に対するコンプレックスもあったのかもしれません。ここ10年ほどのあいだに来日した外国人のなかには「日本人の髪は黒じゃなかったのか？」と驚く人も多くいます。

Q なぜ、日本の大学生は勉強しないのですか？

アメリカの大学は入学しやすく卒業が難しいと言われるのに対して、日本の大学は入学するのが難しく卒業するのは簡単だと言われています。そのため日本では、小学生のうちから睡眠時間を削らなければならないほどの

A Matter of Generation

■ Why do young people dye their hair brown?

Japanese hair is naturally black, of course, but since the 1990s the trend has been to dye it brown. Naturally, each age has its own trends in hair styles and clothing, but there has never been a time when dyeing the hair has gone to this extreme. Even in global terms, it must be somewhat unusual.

Through the 1980s, dyeing the hair was considered to be a special fashion statement, but beginning in the 1990s it became more mainstream. By the mid-1990s, a high ratio of young people were dyeing their hair.

The fact that men were also doing it set this trend apart from the rest. A new word for "brown hair" was invented, *chapatsu*, and became widely accepted. And by the end of the 1990s it was no longer unusual to see middle-aged people with brown hair.

Some explained their preference by saying, "Black hair has a kind of heavy feeling and is sort of tacky, while brown hair makes you feel lighter." There is a possibility, on the other hand, that underlying the whole fad is an inferiority complex toward the way Westerners look. In the last ten years or so, some foreigners coming to Japan have expressed surprise at all the brown hair and said, "Why, I thought Japanese had black hair!"

■ Why don't Japanese university students study?

It is often said that, on the one hand, it is easy to get into American universities but hard to graduate, and on the other hand, it is hard to get into Japanese universities but easy to graduate. It is definitely true that, from childhood on, Japanese students must give their all

受験勉強が課せられます。

いい企業に就職するためにはいい大学を卒業しなくてはならないからです。そのかわり一度入ってしまえば、大学で何を学んだかはほとんど問われません。

そこで大学に入るまでは必死で勉強するかわりに、入学してしまうと気がゆるんで遊んでしまうのです。中には何のために勉強するのかの目的が見出せず、ノイローゼになる人もいます。

すべての大学や大学生を一律に括って語ることはできませんが、学業に熱心ではない学生が多いことについては、講義に出席するだけで単位がとれるようになっているシステム上の問題や、教授たちのレベルを疑問視する声も出ています。

Qなぜ、「お見合い」で結婚できるのですか？

「お見合い」は江戸時代に庶民のあいだで生まれた習慣ですが、第２次世界大戦前には、結婚の約７割がお見合いによるものになっていました。当時の日本は、未婚の男女の恋愛がオープンでなかったうえに、家柄というものを重要視していたので、恋愛結婚が少なかったのです。

しかし戦後、急激にこの傾向に変化があらわれていき、1960年代末には恋愛結婚の比率が見合い結婚を上回り、現在では見合い結婚の比率は全体の10%を下回るようにまでなっています。

ただ最近は、「結婚相談所」などという個人登録制の結婚相手紹介サービスが注目されています。これは、結婚相手に対して、容姿、収入、職種などで高い希望を持つようになっているため、希望が釣り合う男女が出会えるようにするための商業的なお見合いです。また、結婚相手を探すことを目的として一定の条件の男女を集める「カップリング・パーティー」なども開かれるようになっています。

for the university entrance exams, even if it means cutting back on sleeping time.

The reason is that without graduating from a good college, they can't get hired by a good company. However, once they have been employed, it makes little difference what they studied at school.

While students study like crazy to get into college, once there, they relax and take it easy. Some students, having lost the reason why they were studying in the first place, get neurotic.

It is not fair to speak of the various universities and their students as if they were all the same. However, given that many students seem uninterested in their studies, some critics have raised questions about the competence of university teachers and about a system that makes it easy for students to get credit for a class just by showing up.

■ Why do Japanese have arranged marriages?

Arranged marriages came into being among the commoner class during the Edo period (1600-1868). Before World War II, about 70 percent of all marriages were arranged. At the time, unmarried young men and women couldn't associate freely, and the family was considered to be of prime importance. This resulted in their being only a small number of love matches (or love marriages).

In the postwar period, however, things changed radically, and by the end of the 1960s the number of love matches outnumbered arranged marriages. At present, arranged marriages make up less than 10 percent of all marriages.

Recently, however, marriage agencies have appeared which introduce possible marriage partners after the individuals in question have gone through a registration procedure. In effect, this business enables arranged marriages between partners who meet each other's requirements in terms of physical appearance, income, job description, and so on. There are also what are known as "coupling parties," at which men and women who satisfy certain requirements gather to meet potential marriage partners.

なぜ、結婚しない人が増えているのですか？

国勢調査によれば、1950年から80年頃までは、20～34歳の未婚率は、男性で約50%、女性で33%前後と一定していました。それが、80年代後半からこの傾向に大きな変化が見られはじめ、2000年には男性で68.2%、女性で55.5%にまで増えています。

晩婚化が進んでいる理由としては、進学率が高くなっていることや女性の社会参加が挙げられますが、これは世界共通の現象でしょう。

日本特有の理由としては、「結婚すれば自由に使えるお金が減ってしまう」「やりたいことが制約される」といった理由が挙げられています。

それでも、「生涯独身で暮らす」という考えを持っている人は、最近の調査でも、男女ともに５%前後となっているので、いつかは結婚しようと考えている人はそれほど減っていない事実がわかります。

なぜ、子供をあまりつくらないのですか？

これもやはり世界的な傾向になっていることですが、日本でも近年とくに「少子化」が問題視されています。年間の出生数は1973年以降、減少傾向が続いていて、1971年には2.16だった出生率が2003年にはその約60%の1.29にまで落ちています。

晩婚化、未婚化が進めば、少子化も進むのは当然です。また、個人の仕事や生活を重視するライフスタイルが定着していることも大きな要因になっています。さらに終身雇用制度が崩れて、年金制度が揺らいでいる社会事情から、将来の生活に対する不安が生まれてきていることも、少子化が進んでいる事実と無関係ではないでしょう。

■ Why is the number of people who don't marry on the increase?

According to census figures, from 1950 into the 1980s, the percentage of unmarried people in the twenty to thirty-four age category held steady at approximately 50 percent for men and about 33 percent for women. In the latter half of the 1980s, however, a huge change began to take place, and by the year 2000 the figure for men stood at 68.2 percent and for women at 55.5 percent.

Possible reasons for this trend are the increasing number of women getting a higher education and playing a greater role in society. The same phenomenon can be seen elsewhere in the world.

Among the reasons given particularly by Japanese are the following: "If I get married, I'll have less money to spend on my own" and "I'll be restricted in the things I want to do."

That doesn't mean, however, that these people want to remain single for life. According to a recent survey, only around 5 percent want to stay single for life. In other words, the truth is that the number of people who want to get married hasn't declined that much.

■ Why do Japanese have so few children?

This is a worldwide trend, but recently the low birth rate in Japan has become an issue of special concern. Annual childbirths have been declining since 1973, with the 2.16 birth rate of 1971 dropping about 60 percent to 1.29 in 2003.

With the increase of those who marry late or stay single, it is only natural that the birth rate should decline. Another big factor is the firm establishment of lifestyles that focus on the individual's work and social life. There are also such social factors as the collapse of lifetime employment and the shaky condition of the pension system. These naturally lead to an uneasiness about one's future livelihood, which is probably not entirely unconnected to the drop in the birth rate.

Qなぜ、大人も漫画を読むのですか？

たしかに電車の中で熟年の人までが漫画を読んでいる光景は、外国人にとってビックリするものでしょう。

日本における漫画ブームは、1959年に『少年マガジン』と『少年サンデー』という週刊漫画雑誌が同時に創刊されたときから始まりました。そして、はげしい競争の中でひとつの画期的な方式ができあがりました。それは原作者がストーリーを考え、漫画家が絵を描くという「分業制」でした。

たしかに、手塚治虫のように絵もうまく面白いストーリーも考えられる漫画家はいましたが、そのような天才はそんなに多くはいません。

この分業制によって漫画で描かれるテーマは飛躍的にひろがり、漫画誌の読者層も小学生から中学生、高校生、そして大学生へとひろがっていったのです。さらに、大人でも楽しめるストーリーと絵柄で構成された「劇画」というジャンルも生まれました。

『少年ジャンプ』という漫画週刊誌などは一時、発行部数が600万部を超えたほどで、現在ではアメリカやドイツでも発行されています。

さらに1980年前後には、対象を一般男性に向けた成年向け漫画誌が相次いで創刊されました。もちろん、その間には少女漫画誌から成人女性向け漫画誌も成長を見せています。

このようにすべての世代や性別に合わせた漫画誌が刊行されているため、漫画から「卒業」することなく、いつまでも自分に合った漫画を読むようになっていったのです。

■ Why is it that adults also read manga?

It is understandable, I suppose, that foreigners should be surprised when they see men who are no longer young reading manga on the train.

The manga craze began in 1959 with the simultaneous publication of the weekly manga magazines *Shōnen Magajin* and *Shōnen Sandē*. Amidst the furious competition for readership, a revolutionary way of producing manga was developed. It consisted of dividing the responsibilities for producing the manga between the artist who did the drawings and the writer who created the stories.

At the time, there were manga artists like Osamu Tezuka who could both draw well and create an interesting story, but such people were unusual.

Thanks to this system, possible subjects for manga increased tremendously, and manga readership grew beyond the elementary school market to include junior high, high school, and even university students. Next came a type of manga known as *gekiga*, in which both the stories and the artwork could be appreciated by adults.

At one point the weekly manga magazine *Shōnen Jampu* was regularly printing over 6,000,000 copies, and it is now published in local versions in the United States and Germany.

Then around 1980, manga magazines for adult men came out one after another. At the same time, manga aimed at women, from young girls to grown adults, were also evolving.

This is how manga for all generations and both sexes came into being, meaning that one never "outgrows" manga but can always find something that suits one's taste.

なぜ、Q 「団塊の世代」が注目されているのですか？

「団塊の世代」とは、第2次世界大戦後の1947年から49年に生まれた世代を指しています（終戦は1945年）。第1次ベビーブームに当たるこの期間には約800万人が誕生しています。戦争のために人口が減少していたあとのベビーブームだったため、この世代の人口分布は、前後の年齢層にくらべても厚くなっています。

戦後、さまざまな価値観が大きく変容していく中で育ち、高度経済成長を遂げたあとの日本経済を支えるとともに、多くの流行や風潮をつくってきた世代と位置付けられます。そうしたことからも、戦前生まれの世代や、高度成長期以降に生まれた世代とは価値観が異なっている部分もあるのでしょう。

日本の会社では60歳か61歳の定年制を敷いているので、この人たちが2007年から退職していきます。これほど大きな影響力を持つパワフルな世代が退職してから何をするのか、また社会はどう変わっていくのか、ということで注目されているのです。

なぜ、Q 「熟年離婚」が増えているのですか？

1970年には婚姻件数全体の約10％に過ぎなかった離婚件数が、2000年には約30％に達しているように、近年、急激に離婚が増加しています。かつては「離婚＝良くないこと」という社会通念がありましたが、それが少しずつ薄れてきています。

とくに多いのは若い層の離婚ですが、それとともに中高年夫婦の離婚がここ10年で2倍以上に増えていて、これが「熟年離婚」と呼ばれる社会問題になっています。子供の成人や夫の定年退職を機に妻側から離婚を申し出るケースが多いと言われています。日本では、子供が誕生すると、妻には「母親としての役割」が当てはめ

■ Why is the first generation of Japanese baby boomers attracting so much attention now?

The first generation of Japanese baby boomers, born in the postwar years from 1947 to the end of 1949 (the war ended in 1945), is referred to as the *dankai* generation (*dankai* meaning something like "clump"). About 8,000,000 people were born into this first generation of baby boomers. This generation appeared after a decrease in population during the war, so it stands out for its size.

The *dankai* generation grew up in the postwar period when values were going through great changes. It became the main driving force behind the Japanese economy following the postwar high-growth period, which started around the mid 1950s. At the same time, the *dankai* created many social fads and vogues. It stands to reason that this generation should be somewhat different from the generations born before the war and the generations born after the period of high economic growth.

The retirement age for most companies in Japan is sixty or sixty-one, so the *dankai* generation will start retiring in 2007. The big question is what will this very influential generation do then, after it stops working? What changes will take place in society? These questions are attracting a lot of attention.

■ Why is middle-age divorce increasing?

In 1970 only about 10 percent of all marriages ended in divorce, but recently this number has reached about 30 percent, showing a rapid increase in the number of divorces. Not too long ago divorce was socially frowned upon, but that attitude has slowly begun to wear thin.

Divorce among the young is particularly common, but divorce among the middle-aged has also doubled in the last ten years, becoming a social problem. It is said that in many cases the wife seeks a divorce when the children have grown up or the husband reaches retirement. In Japan, when children are born, the wife is caught up in performing her "duty as a mother." But it seems that

られがちなため、一定の役割を終えたときに「個人としての人生」を見直してみたいと考える女性が増えているのでしょう。

2007年から団塊の世代が定年を迎えるようになるため、熟年離婚はさらに増えていくのではないかと予想されています。

once this duty is finished, many women want to take another look at their life as an individual.

It is predicted that when the first generation of baby boomers (the *dankai* generation) reaches retirement, starting in 2007, there will be another increase in the number of divorces of middle-aged couples.

9 マナー

Qなぜ、握手ではなくお辞儀をするのですか？

握手には手に武器を持っていないことを示す意味があり、お辞儀には自分の首を差し出すことで敵意がないのを示す意味があるとも言われているので、その起源は似ているのかもしれません。

ただし、握手は親睦や和解の表現、お辞儀は相手への敬意をあらわす表現として行われるとも考えられているように、「意味合い」としては違った要素を持つ挨拶だとは言えるでしょう。

明治維新(1868年)以降、日本では西洋の文化を積極的に受け入れてきましたが、握手に関してだけはなかなか馴染みにくかったようです。今でも見知らぬ人や異性の手を気軽に握ることには抵抗感があります。最近では外国人相手なら違和感なく握手することができるようになりましたが、挨拶としての抱擁やキスが自然にできるようになるまでにはまだ時間がかかりそうです。

Qなぜ、「正座」が正しい座り方なのですか？

正座は、それほど古くから根付いていたわけではありません。かつて正座は「かしこまる」「つくばう」と呼ばれ、神前や仏前、茶室などにおける儀式的な場面で用いられる程度でした。16世紀末まではあぐらや立て膝で座っていたのです。それが江戸時代（1600-1868）になって、全国の大名が将軍に拝謁する際、1人に与えられた畳1畳の上で正座をするのが礼儀となり、これが全国に広まったと言われています。

Social Behavior

■ Why do Japanese bow rather than shake hands?

It is said that the act of shaking hands in the West shows that you are not carrying a weapon, while bowing in Japan—that is, stretching out your head and neck toward the other person—shows that you are a friend and not an enemy. In this sense, the two acts may have similar roots.

However, the two greetings are different in that handshaking indicates friendliness and is an attempt to establish good relations, while bowing is an expression of respect for the other party.

From the beginning of the Meiji period (1868-1912), Japan was quick to adopt many elements of Western culture, but the handshake was something that Japanese couldn't quite get used to. Even in fairly recent times Japanese did not feel comfortable in casually taking the hand of someone they didn't know, or someone of the opposite sex. These days, if the other party is a foreigner, we can shake hands without feeling uncomfortable, but it will undoubtedly be a while before we can greet people with a hug or a kiss in a natural way.

■ Why is *seiza* considered the correct way to sit?

The *seiza* style of sitting does not have a long history. At first, it was called *kashikomaru* or *tsukubau* and was only practiced at Shintō or Buddhist ceremonies and at tea ceremonies. Until the end of the sixteenth century, the proper way to sit was in the *agura* or *tatehiza* style. Things changed in the Edo period (1600-1868) when local lords (*daimyō*) had to appear before the shogun. It then became the custom for these lords to sit in the *seiza* style on a single tatami mat, and this style spread throughout the country.

明治時代になってからは、学校教育としても正しい座り方として正座を指導するようになりました。狭いスペースで、足の痛みをこらえるというように、慎み深さと忍耐強さが求められる点でも、日本人には美徳として捉えられた部分が大きかったのでしょう。日本の家庭でも畳とちゃぶ台の生活が一般化していく中で、食事をする際にも正座をしていることが正しいマナーとして定着していきました。

ただ、畳が少なくなり、テーブルとイスの生活が主流になっている現在、1時間以上正座を続けられる日本人は10人に1人もいないのではないでしょうか。

Qなぜ、子供をもっと叱らないのですか？

電車の中などの公共の場所で、子供が騒いでいても注意をしない親たちは増えています。武家社会が続いていた頃や、近代から昭和（1926-1989）の初期までは厳しいしつけが行われており、子供であっても他人に迷惑をかけるような行為は強くとがめられていましたが、そんな状況が近年大きく変わりだしています。

その要因を一点だけに絞ることはできませんが、第2次世界大戦における敗戦も大きかったのでしょう。これによって、日本人の従来の価値観が大きく揺らぎ、それまで信じていた親の教え、学校の教え、国の教えに対する自信を喪失し、子供に対するしつけを厳しくできなくなったと指摘されています。

1980年代中頃、成熟した大人としての自覚と責任を拒否している世代という意味も持つ「新人類」という言葉が誕生しました。その新人類が今度は親になり、祖父母にもなりつつあるわけですから、その傾向が強まっていくのも無理はありません。

In the Meiji period, *seiza* was taught in schools as the proper way to sit. *Seiza* calls for one to sit in a small space, bear the pain from uncomfortably positioned legs, but at the same time show a strong will and a sense of respect. All of this probably appealed to the Japanese idea of what was right and proper at that time, and Japanese households increasingly took their meals while sitting in the *seiza* style on tatami flooring before a low table (*chabudai*). This came to be considered correct etiquette.

Today, with tatami flooring getting rarer and chairs and tables appearing in its place, I doubt that one out of ten Japanese could bear to sit in the *seiza* style for even one hour.

■ Why aren't children scolded more when they do something wrong?

More and more, parents these days don't scold their children even when the children are acting up on the train or in some other public place. Back when society was dominated by the samurai class, and even in modern times up to the beginning of the Shōwa period (1926-1989), children were made to behave properly. They were not allowed to cause trouble for other people, regardless of their age. Today, however, the situation has changed dramatically.

It is impossible to point out just one reason for this change, but Japan's defeat in World War II is undoubtedly a big factor. As some have pointed out, Japan's defeat shook the country's traditional value system to its foundations. People lost confidence in what their parents taught them, in what the schools taught them, and in what the government told them. As a result, they lost confidence in their ability to discipline their children.

In the mid 1980s a "new breed" of young people reached maturity who refused to look upon themselves as mature adults with social responsibilities. That "new breed" have now become parents themselves and will soon become grandparents. It should come as no surprise if the lack of discipline becomes even more common.

Qなぜ、チップを渡さないのですか？

ヨーロッパでもチップに対する考え方はかなり曖昧になっていて、チップがほぼ制度化しているのはアメリカだけのようです。チップを出し忘れたときには、「何かサービスにまずいところがありましたか？」と問われることも珍しくありません。また、チップの相場が変動しているのも困りもので、10%を払えばいいという知識でチップを払うと、「なぜ15%出さないのか」と言われることもあります。

アメリカではチップが給料の一部と捉えられていますが、日本にはそうしたシステムはありません。アメリカ人にとっても、チップをいくら出すかというのは悩みの種のようで、日本のノーチップ制を「天国にいるようだ」と喜ぶ人もいるほどです。

Qなぜ、どこでもおしぼりを使うのですか？

日本の飲食店で、おしぼりを出す店は60%以上にもなるそうです。おしぼりの起源は、江戸時代の旅館で、疲れた旅人に出したことだといわれ、1970年代に飲食店のサービスとして定着していきました。食事の前に手を拭いておくのは衛生的にも好ましいためか、最近では、海外の航空会社などでも取り入れられてきました。

日本では、ナプキンやフィンガー・ボールを使う習慣がありませんから、食事のとき指先を拭くというためにも必需品となっています。

Qなぜ、店員に挨拶を返さないのですか？

お店で、店員が「いらっしゃいませ」と挨拶しているのに客のほうは何も言葉を返さないことが、外国の人には不思議に見えるようです。では、「いらっしゃいま

■ Why don't Japanese tip service workers?

The attitude toward tipping varies in Europe. The United States seems to be the only country where the system is firmly established. If you don't tip in the United States, it is not unusual to be asked if there was something wrong with the service. A further complication is that the proper amount can vary, so if you tip 10 percent, you might be asked why you didn't tip 15 percent.

In the United States, the tip is considered part of the salary, but in Japan, of course, there is no such system. Even Americans worry about the proper amount to tip, and so they are quite happy to hear that there is no tipping in Japan.

■ Why are oshibori (wet hand towels) so common?

Statistically, over 60 percent of Japanese restaurants and other eating and drinking establishments provide customers with a wet hand towel (either hot or cold) to wipe their hands before eating. These oshibori are said to have originated in the Edo period (1600-1868), when inns provided them to tired travelers. This custom became firmly established in the 1970s wherever food was served. Since it is undoubtedly a good practice to wipe the hands before eating, many foreign airlines have recently begun to provide oshibori as part of their service.

Since Japanese do not have the custom of using napkins or finger bowls, the oshibori has become a necessary item during meals to keep one's fingers clean.

■ Why don't Japanese respond when greeted by a store clerk?

Visitors to Japan seem to think it odd that when a Japanese enters a store and is welcomed by a clerk, who says, *Irasshaimase*, the cus-

せ」と言われて、どう返事すればいいかというと、その言葉が日本語にはないのです。たとえば店員から「おはようございます」と言われれば「おはようございます」と返すでしょうし、食事後には客側から自発的に「ごちそうさま」と声をかける場合もよくあります。個人差はあることですが、店員に対してどうしても挨拶をしたくないわけではありません。

日本では、店員は客に対して必要以上に馴れ馴れしくしないで、敬語や丁寧語を用いながら接するのがマナーとされています。タクシーに乗った際でも、親しげに話しかけてくる運転手に対し、会話をはずませる客もいれば、不快感を抱く人もいるように、これはやはり個人差がある問題です。

こうした反応は、客と店員の間に上下関係を感じるかどうかにかかっています。アメリカでは平等に会話しますが、イギリスでは客に敬意を表して「サー」をつけます。

日本はアメリカとイギリスの中間くらいと言えるのかもしれません。

Qなぜ、国歌を歌うときに起立しない人がいるのですか？

2001年9月11日に同時多発テロ事件が起きたあと、アメリカでは多くの星条旗が掲げられたように、国旗や国歌は愛国心の象徴になるものです。また、国旗を掲げて国家を歌う際には、起立して姿勢を正すのは、国民として当然の態度だとも言えるでしょう。

しかし日本では、「日の丸」を国旗とし、「君が代」を国歌とする法律が定められたのが1999年のことで、その後も、国旗掲揚や国歌斉唱を義務付けていいのかが裁判で争われたりするような不自然な事態が起きています。

tomer doesn't respond. As it happens, *Irassahimase* is a greeting that doesn't require a response—for which, in fact, no customary response exists in the Japanese language. Literally, *Irasshaimase* is a polite form of the verb meaning "come"; loosely, it can be translated as "Welcome!" On the other hand, if the clerk says "Good morning" in Japanese, the customer may respond with a "Good morning." At restaurants, customers often compliment the staff on the quality of the meal.

When taking a taxi, if the cabby is very friendly, some people respond by being friendly in return, while others might show clearly that they aren't interested in conversation. While there are differences among individuals in each of these situations, it is more than simply preferring not to exchange greetings with clerks. In general, the Japanese view is that clerks should use polite, respectful language when speaking with customers and not be overly friendly.

The relationship between customers and clerks depends on whether they see themselves as being on an equal footing or whether the customer is seen as being superior to the clerk. In the United States, the relationship is equal, but in Great Britain the customer is seen as being the superior party and addressed appropriately as "sir" or "madam."

Japan can perhaps be seen as falling somewhere in between.

■ Why do some Japanese refuse to stand when the national anthem is played?

After the terrorist attacks of September 11, 2001, many Americans displayed the American flag as a symbol of patriotism. Another symbol of patriotism, of course, is a country's national anthem. And it can be said that standing at attention as the anthem is played and the flag is raised is the natural behavior of every citizen.

In Japan, the national flag and anthem were not legally adopted until 1999. In fact, strangely enough, a case is currently before the courts to decide whether citizens can be legally forced to honor the raising of the flag and singing of the anthem.

こうした問題の背景には、第２次世界大戦で敗れるまでの日本では、「日の丸」や「君が代」が皇国思想や軍国主義思想の精神的支柱になっていたという事実があります。

そのため、「日の丸」や「君が代」が何を象徴しているのかが問われ、国旗や国歌に対する姿勢までを規定することが、憲法で定められている「思想・信条の自由」に反するのではないかという意見が出ています。

つまり、マナーの問題だけではなく、思想の問題として、国旗や国歌に対する姿勢が分かれているわけです。

Qなぜ、「大和魂」という言葉がよく使われるのですか？

直訳すれば「日本人の精神」となる大和魂という言葉はもともと、1000年以上も前に中国などから新しい知識や学問が入ってきたときに、日本人固有の考え方に合わせて応用しながら取り入れようとする実務的能力を指すものでした。それが、江戸時代からは「日本人固有の心」という意味を持つようになり、第２次世界大戦中にはナショナリズムを象徴した言葉にもなっています。そうした変遷を考えると、この言葉が何を示しているかは、かなり曖昧だとも言えるわけです。

最近では、「簡単にはあきらめないファイティングスピリット」といった意味までが付加されているようで、むしろそうした意味での使用法が多くなっています。そのため国際スポーツ大会の場で聞かれることが多く、「サムライ・スピリット」に似た意味を持つ言葉として用いられているようです。

Qなぜ、受話器に向かってお辞儀をするのですか？

電話で話をしていて、相手が目の前にいないのに、ぺこぺこ頭を下げながら謝っている光景はたしかに見かけられます。それでも、最近ではそれほど頻繁なことでは

At the root of this problem is the fact that the flag and anthem were used as spiritual supports for Japanese imperialism and nationalism during World War II.

The question is what the flag and anthem now symbolize, and whether the Japanese people can be forced to honor them without infringing upon the freedoms of thought and religion as guaranteed in the constitution.

Thus the difference in opinion concerning the flag and national anthem did not arise from simple questions about proper behavior or etiquette, but from concerns about the freedom of thought.

■ Why do I hear the words "Yamato-damashii" so often during sporting events?

Literally, Yamato-damashii means something close to "Japanese spirit." It came into use over a thousand years ago when new types of scholarship and learning came to Japan from China and Korea. The idea was that this new learning would be adopted and combined with Japanese pragmatism, which would be represented by the phrase Yamato-damashii. During the Edo period (1600-1868), the phrase came to be identified with the indigenous Japanese ways of thinking — the heart and soul of being Japanese. In this sense, it became a symbol of Japanese nationalism during World War II. Given this background, one must admit that the meaning of Yamato-damashii is not all that clear.

Recently the meaning "unfaltering fighting spirit" has been added to the mix, and this usage has gotten more common. One hears it more and more during international sporting events, and the meaning has grown quite close to "samurai spirit."

■ Why do Japanese bow when on the telephone?

It's true that you sometimes see people talking on the phone, and even though there is no one there to bow to, the person is bowing rapidly and apologizing for one thing or another. However, this is

なくなり、日本人であってもこうした光景を見かければ、滑稽な仕草として受け止めるようにもなっています。

ただし、たとえ相手が目の前にいなくても、本心で何を考えているのかは、言葉のトーンなどで相手に伝わることもあります。そのため、「相手が目の前にいるつもりで態度に気をつけて、お辞儀をするくらいの気持ちで話をするのが電話の心がけ」というマナー教育を受けることは今でもあるようです。

「日本人は本音と建前を使い分ける」と言われていることにも関係するのでしょうが、ちょっとした表情や態度から、相手が心の中で何を考えているかを窺おうとする傾向が見られます。相手が目の前にいなくても、常に真剣な態度で向かい合おうとする姿勢は、そうした背景から生まれているのかもしれません。

not as common as it used to be, and even Japanese have come to see it as a little humorous.

Yet, even when a person is not right in front of you, there still may be something in your tone of voice that lets him or her know what you are really thinking. Apparently even today, wherever telephone etiquette is taught, the basics consist of being as careful in your attitude as if the other party were actually in front of you, and expressing yourself with as much feeling as you would if you were actually bowing.

This phenomenon might be connected to the fact that Japanese distinguish between what they think and what they need to say to meet social expectations. Many Japanese will therefore try to guess what the other party is really thinking from the slightest expression or smallest gesture. This habit may give rise to the situations discussed here, where even though there is no one physically in front of them, Japanese still try to show how sincere they are through their bodily movements.

10 性（セックス）

なぜ、Q 街中にヌード雑誌が氾濫しているのですか？

多くの点において保守的な傾向が強い日本ですが、テレビや雑誌における暴力やセックスに対する表現への規制は、欧米にくらべてゆるやかです。

以前の日本では、性器や陰毛を露出した写真や映像の公開は全面的に禁じられ、摘発の対象になっていました。それが、1991年に女優の陰毛が写っている写真集が出版されても摘発されなかったのを皮切りに、なし崩しに「ヘア解禁」状態ができあがりました。

この背景には、芸術的な色合いが強い海外映画作品を、陰毛が露出しているというだけの理由で上映を禁止し、それに対して海外から強い反発があったことがあげられます。しかし、性器そのものが写っている写真や映像の公開は、ごく一部の例外を除いて現在でも禁じられています。

日本では一流の週刊誌がヌード写真を載せたり、一流の新聞が露骨な性描写が頻出する小説を載せたりしますが、これは世界でもあまり見られない現象で、こんなことも「ヌードが氾濫している」というイメージを与えているのでしょう。

なぜ、Q 相撲や祭りなどでは、褌姿になれるのですか？

古来、日本人は性に対して開放的でした。日本の国がどのようにして出来たかということを伝える神話には、性にまつわるエピソードがたくさん出てきます。

ですから、日本の祭りには「裸祭」といったものや、性のシンボルを中心にした祭りも数多くあります。相撲

Sexual Matters

■ Why are there so many nude magazines sold openly?

Japan is conservative in many ways, but when it comes to restrictions on violence and nudity in magazines and on television, it is not as strict as the United States or Europe.

In the past, exposure of genitals and pubic hair in photographs and movies for public consumption was completely banned and subject to police action. In 1991, however, a collection of photographs showing the pubic hair of a well-known actress was published, and since no legal action was taken, open season on pubic hair gradually came into being.

As to why this happened, one factor was the previous banning of very artistic foreign movies that showed pubic hair, which produced a strong foreign reaction. However, even now, with very few exceptions, photographs and movies for public consumption that show the genitals in plain view are still banned.

There are not many countries other than Japan where respected magazines carry nude photographs, and respected newspapers serialize novels filled with explicit sexual scenes. I suppose that produces the impression that nudity is more widespread than it really is.

■ Why do Japanese men dress in nothing but loincloths in Sumo tournaments and at festivals?

In ancient times, Japanese were more open regarding sex. In the myths that depict the origins of the country, there are many episodes relating to sex.

Consequently, in some Japanese festivals, the men wear nothing

も古来神事として行われてきたので、裸に近い格好なのです。

祭りにおいて、褌姿でお神輿を担いでいる姿などは、ダンディに近い意味を持つ「粋」とされ、男らしさの象徴と見られます。とくに博多の山笠や浅草の三社祭などは、その地域における１年間でもっとも注目される行事になっているので、これに参加することは個人としての誇りになっています。

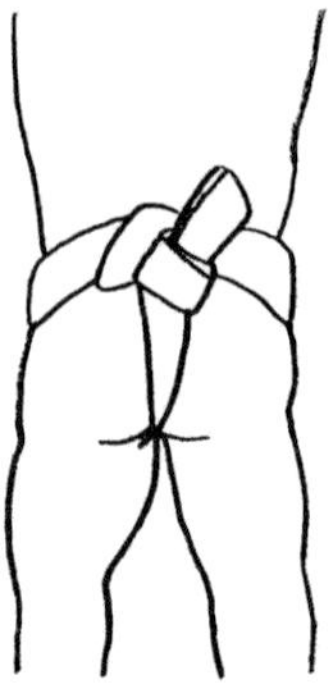

ブラジル人がリオのカーニバルに参加するのと、感覚としては似ているのかもしれません。日本人がカーニバルを見れば、女性たちが半裸に近い姿で踊っていることが不思議に思えるものです。

なぜ、Q 歌舞伎では男性が女役をやるのですか？

日本特有の演劇である歌舞伎の起源は、出雲阿国という女性が、歌舞伎者といわれる異様な風体をした男性たちの姿やふるまいを取り入れた「かぶき踊り」を始めたことにあります。これは17世紀はじめのことですが、その後はこれを模倣した遊女歌舞伎や若衆歌舞伎が流行しました。

ただ、これらの興行は性的な連想を抱かせるものであったり、実際に売色行為を兼ねていたものであったことから、風紀紊乱を理由に禁止されました。そこで、すべての役柄を男優が演じる現在の歌舞伎が生まれたのです。

庶民の娯楽として発展した歌舞伎ですが、その後にさまざまな様式が整えられて日本文化を象徴する芸能となり、2005年には世界無形文化遺産にも選ばれています。

but loincloths (these are called "naked festivals"), while other festivals are centered around sexual symbols. Sumo wrestling was originally looked upon as a religious ceremony, which explains why the men are close to being naked.

Carrying one of the portable shrines in a festival dressed only in a loincloth is seen as being dandyish, cool, and the ultimate symbol of manhood. Particularly at festivals like the Yamagasa Festival in Hakata and the Sanja Festival in Asakusa, which are the most important events of the year for the local communities, people are proud to take part.

I suppose this is how Brazilians feel when they take part in the carnival in Rio de Janeiro. Ironically, when Japanese see women dancing in a nearly naked state in this carnival, they don't see it as equivalent of their naked festivals but rather as something extraordinary.

■ Why are the women's roles in Kabuki played by men?

The history of Kabuki began when a woman named Okuni (or Izumo no Okuni) began dancing something called the Kabuki dance, in which she had incorporated the outlandish costumes and actions of young men about town called *kabuki-mono*. This was at the beginning of the seventeenth century. Not long afterward, this dance was successfully imitated by other groups consisting of prostitutes or young men.

However, since these productions were explicitly sexual, or were in actual fact directly connected to the selling of sex, they were banned as being harmful to public morals. This is when the forerunner of Kabuki as we know it today came into being, with men playing both male and female roles.

As the theater of the common man, Kabuki continued to develop and evolve, eventually becoming one of the representative arts of Japanese culture. In 2005 UNESCO named it one of the Masterpieces of the Oral and Intangible Heritage of Humanity.

なぜ、銭湯（公衆浴場）で、みんなが裸でいられるのですか？

外国にはシャワーだけでもいいという人が多いのに対し、日本人はお湯につかることが習慣となっています。夏は高温多湿で冬は寒い気候の問題などが理由に挙げられますが、昔から日本人には風呂好きが多いのです。

それにもかかわらず、設備的な問題もあり、各家庭にお風呂が設けられるようになったのは、第２次世界大戦以降の高度成長期に入った1960年代からでした。それ以前は、銭湯という公衆浴場を利用する以外にお風呂に入ることはできなかったわけです。

銭湯の起源は12世紀にまで遡りますが、現在の銭湯に近い公衆浴場は17世紀頃から広まっていきました。そして、家庭にお風呂が普及するまでは、町ごとにある銭湯が地域の社交場としての役割も果たしていたのです。

そうした交流がほんの40年ほど前は日常的になされていたのですから、銭湯で裸になることに抵抗を持たない人が多いのも当然です。ただ、最近では銭湯に行った経験がない子供たちが増えているため、修学旅行などで水着をつけてお風呂に入るケースも出てきています。

なぜ、掃除のおばさんの前で用を足すことができるのですか？

駅や空港、デパートなどのトイレで、女性清掃員が作業している傍で男性が用を足しているのが外国人には驚きのようです。これもやはり銭湯と関係があるのかもしれません。銭湯では入り口に番台があり、そこで店側の人が料金を受け取るとともに、プールの監視員のような役割を果たしています。

外国の人はどうして異性の前で裸になれるのかと驚くようですが、システムの問題として受け入れるしかないわけです。トイレの清掃員もそうです。

■ Why don't Japanese feel embarrassed about stripping naked at a public bath?

In some countries, many people seem to be satisfied with taking a shower, but in Japan it's customary to take a hot bath. Many reasons can be given for this, such as the hot muggy weather in summer and the cold weather in winter, but whatever the reason, it is true that Japanese have liked hot baths since the distant past.

Nevertheless, perhaps due to manufacturing difficulties, it was not until the postwar economic boom centering on the 1960s that baths came to be a part of people's homes. Before that, there was no choice but to go to a public bath.

The origins of the public bath go back as far as the twelfth century, but it was not until around the seventeenth century that something resembling the modern public bath began to spread. From then until individual homes came to have their own baths, the public bath served both as a bath and as a gathering place for local communities all over the country.

This was a part of everyday life until just forty short years ago, so there are still a lot of people who don't feel embarrassed about stripping naked at the public bath. But since the number of children who have never been to a public bath is on the increase, some children, when on a school outing, put on bathing suits before going to the public bath.

■ Why is it that Japanese men can use a urinal while a older cleaning woman is working nearby?

Many visitors to Japan are surprised when they see Japanese men standing at urinals at train stations, airports, and department stores while an older cleaning woman is working nearby. This phenomenon could have a connection with the tradition of the public bath. At the entrance to the bathing area there is sort of a podium where an attendant sits. It is the attendant's job to take money from customers and to keep an eye on the bathers.

Foreigners wonder how it is possible to strip naked and bathe in

日本の男性は年配の女性を母親的存在と受け止め、異性と意識しない傾向が強いのかもしれません。

Q なぜ、日本人はセックスの回数が少ないのですか？

イギリスのヘルスケア会社が実施した調査によると、日本人の年間セックス回数は45回で、調査した41カ国中で最少だったそうです。トップはギリシア人で138回。前年にトップだったフランスは6位に落ちて120回。世界の平均は103回といいますから、半分にもなりません。

また最近の調査によると、自分たちはセックスレスだと思う夫婦が50％近くもいることが分かりました。30代と40代で47％、50代50％、60代で51％です。ちなみに、回数は1年以上ない夫婦が34％、3ヵ月に1度、6ヵ月に1度の人がそれぞれ10％とのことです。

その理由としては「面倒くさい」「親との同居」「忙しくて時間がない」「マンネリ化した」などが挙げられていますが、これでは日本が「少子化」するのも無理はないでしょう。

front of someone of the opposite sex, which the attendant might be. In a sense, this is how the system functions, and Japanese realize it has to be accepted as such. The same applies to the cleaning woman. Another factor might be that Japanese men look upon older women as mother figures, not really seeing them as members of the opposite sex.

■ Why do Japanese have so little sex?

According to a survey carried out by a British healthcare organization in 2005, Japanese couples have sex an average of 45 times a year, the lowest among the forty-one countries surveyed. The highest was Greece at 138 times. The previous year's highest, France, had dropped to sixth place at 120 times. The overall average was 103 times, so Japan was not even half of that.

According to a Japanese survey, nearly 50 percent of Japanese couples described themselves as sexless. Couples in their thirties and forties stood at 47 percent; those in their fifties at 50 percent; those in their sixties at 51 percent. Thirty-four percent hadn't had sex for over a year. Those who had sex once every three months stood at 10 percent, as did those who had sex once every six months.

The reasons given were that it was just too much trouble, they were living with their parents, they were too busy, or the freshness had disappeared. All this might help to explain the drop in the Japanese fertility rate.

11 街中で

なぜ、Q こんなにパチンコ屋があるのですか？

パチンコとは、ピンボールとスロットマシーンの要素を併せ持ったようなゲームの一種です。現在、全国には１万5000軒を超すパチンコ店があります。パチンコ店は「風俗営業」に規定されていて、警察の許可を必要とします。パチンコは単なる遊技ではなく、賭博性の高い遊技です。日本では、カジノが認められていないだけでなく、公営競馬などの例外を除けば原則として賭博は禁止されているため、パチンコは「法にとがめられない身近なギャンブル」として人気を博しているのです。

なぜ、パチンコが違法にならないかについては、さまざまな問題が指摘されています。パチンコ店では、ゲームに勝った場合も直接、配当金は得られず、勝った分のパチンコ玉やコインをいったん景品に変えたうえで、パチンコ店の外にある別の施設で換金する形式がとられています。そのため、営業構造上は賭博になっていないと見なされているのです。

なぜ、Q 道にまで植木鉢を置いたりするのですか？

日本で園芸が一般人にまで普及したのは江戸時代(1600-1868)に入ってからです。初代将軍の徳川家康(1542-1616) が花好きであったため、大名・旗本がこぞって追随して珍花や奇木を集めだし、それに伴い、庶民も鉢植えの花を楽しむようになったと言われています。そして当時から、集めた鉢植えをどこに置くかという問題がありました。

日本の住宅事情は今でも決して良くはありませんが、

Around Town

■ Why are there so many pachinko parlors?

Pachinko is a game that combines the features of a pinball machine with those of a slot machine. There are now more than 15,000 pachinko parlors throughout Japan. Since they are considered part of the entertainment and amusement trade, they are required to have a police permit. Pachinko is not just an innocent pastime, however; it is a form of gambling. Casinos are not legal in Japan, and aside from a few exceptions like publicly managed horse racing, gambling of any kind is prohibited. Pachinko has achieved its immense popularity because it is seen as a legal, innocent way of gambling.

As to why pachinko is not considered illegal, there are a number of possible reasons. One is that when you win at pachinko, you do not immediately receive your winnings in the form of cash. First you receive pachinko balls or special coins (tokens) that you exchange for prizes. Then, at a small exchange center outside the pachinko parlor, you can exchange the prizes for money. For this reason, pachinko is not considered a form of organized gambling.

■ Why are there potted plants along roadsides?

It was not until the Edo (or Tokugawa) period (1600-1868) that ordinary people took up gardening. The first Tokugawa shogun, Ieyasu (1542-1616), loved flowers, and lesser lords and retainers all followed his lead in collecting rare flowers and unusual trees. They were followed by the common people, who developed an interest in potted flowers. The problem immediately arose as to where to place these potted plants.

Even now, Japanese housing conditions are not the best. Back

江戸時代にも、棟続きの細長い平家を仕切った「長屋」というアパートに住んでいる人が多かったのです。そんな長屋には庭なんかありませんでした。

長屋の前の狭い道は、そこで洗濯をしたり魚を焼いたりするなど、家の中と変わらないように扱われていたのです。そうしたこともあって、家の前の道は、私道か公道かを問わず、その家に住んでいる人の領域と考えてしまう傾向が強く、そこに植物を置いてしまったのでしょう。現在でも東京の下町の裏通りには、多くの鉢植えが並んでいて、安らぎの空間を作り出しています。

Qなぜ、都市開発は景観を無視しているのですか？

日本の家屋は、西洋とは違って、木と紙でできていました。そのため、ひとたび火事になれば大火になることも多く、火消し（現在の消防隊）は消火にあたるというより、延焼を防ぐために周囲の建物を取り壊していたくらいです。そのように破壊と再生の繰り返しを続けていたため、行き当たりばったりで家を建てるのが当然と考えるようになっていきました。

東京に関していえば、太平洋戦争の大空襲によって焼け野原になったあと、「都市計画のもとに整備された街を創ろう」と発案した政治家もいたのですが、うやむやのうちに人々は手当たり次第に家を建てはじめ、区画整理もままなりませんでした。

役人の多くは、景観が公共の財産という考えを持たず、建築業者の利益を優先した政策をとりつづけたため、現在のような奇怪な景観が作りだされたと言えるでしょう。

ひどい例としては、日本を代表する橋「日本橋」の上に高速道路の屋根をつけてしまったケースが挙げられます。パリの凱旋門の上にモノレールの駅をつくったようなものです。

then, many people in Edo (present-day Tokyo) lived in crowded row houses, which were long, narrow, one-story apartment buildings in which the individual apartments shared a common wall. These row houses didn't have nearly enough space for a yard or garden.

The narrow road in front of the row house was used as though it was part of the building. People did their washing there, grilled fish, and did other household activities. Whether the road was public or private was beside the point; people thought of it as their own territory. I imagine that's why they began putting their potted plants out in the street. Even today, in the backstreets of that part of Tokyo where the common people used to live, you can still see potted plants out in the streets, creating a nice, warm atmosphere.

■ Why does Japanese city planning ignore the landscape?

In contrast to Western housing, traditional Japanese housing consisted of paper and wood. In the past, once a fire broke out, it often spread completely out of control. Rather than trying to put out the fire, firefighters would often just try to keep it from spreading by tearing down houses in its path. As the cycle of tearing down and building up repeated itself, building at random came to be seen as the normal state of affairs.

After Tokyo was reduced to blackened ruins by the American fire bombings at the end of World War II, some politicians proposed that the city be rebuilt according to a well thought-out plan. But without anyone knowing how it happened, houses started going up at random anyway. Any thought of rational planning went out the window.

Most government offices had no idea that scenery, or the cityscape, was part of the national heritage, and therefore promoted policies that gave priority to construction company profits. All of this resulted in the ugly cityscapes that we see today.

As one particularly terrible example, an elevated highway was built over Nihonbashi, a bridge that is one of the symbols of Japan. This is equivalent to building a monorail station over Paris's Arc de Triomphe.

なぜ、Q こんなに占い師が多いのですか？

古代においては、世界的に見ても、政治が占いや神託と結びついていることは多かったのですが、日本ではその風潮が長く続いていました。

もちろん、占いによって政治のすべてを行なっていたわけではありませんが、催事を行なう際はもちろん、都市開発などを行なう際にも、占いや風水による判断は大きな比重を占めていました。そうした意味でいっても、日本人はもともと吉凶を気にする面が強く、占い的なものが好きだったと言えるのでしょう。

現代でも、雑誌などでは、生年月日などから運勢を占うコーナーを設けることが当たり前のようになっています。しかし、そうした占いだけでは飽き足らず、もっと個人的なことに関して、今後の指針を示してもらいたいと考える人たちもいるわけです。そうした需要があるため、占いを職業にしている人は増えてきたのです。

なぜ、Q 秋葉原には電気店がこんなに多いのですか？

東京の秋葉原は「電気街」として有名です。これはもともと、第２次世界大戦後に各地に闇市が形成されていた際、この近くに電機学校があったことから、電子部品を扱う店舗が増えていったのが始まりでした。

ただ、現在の秋葉原は「電気街」としてだけではなく「おたくの町」としても世界的な注目を集めています。これは、秋葉原でパソコンやパソコンソフトを扱う店が増えてきたあと、1990年代後半に「美少女ゲーム」が登場すると、そうしたソフトや関連商品を扱う店が人気になったためです。最近では、電化製品とは関係のない「美少女文化」とでも呼べるようなものが、秋葉原から発信されるようにもなっています。

■ Why are there so many fortune-tellers?

Throughout human history, politics has tended to be closely tied to fortune-telling and oracles. This state of affairs continued for a long time in Japan.

Of course, policies were not entirely formulated based on fortune-telling, but things like special events and city planning did rely heavily on both fortune-telling and feng shui. It seems that Japanese have always been concerned with what their fortune or fate might be, and thus have always had a fondness for fortune-telling.

Today, it is taken for granted that magazines and other printed media will have a section devoted to fortune-telling based on a person's age or some other factor. However, this doesn't completely satisfy some people; they want more personal advice regarding their future. It is this demand that has kept the number of professional fortune-tellers growing.

■ Why are there so many electronics stores in Akihabara?

Tokyo's Akihabara, also known as Electric Town, is famous for its large number of electronics stores. The origins of present-day Akihabara can be found in the black markets that arose after World War II. There was an electrical engineering school near Akihabara, and as a natural result, black-market stores dealing in electrical parts began to set up shop near the school. This was the beginning of Akihabara's Electric Town.

Now, however, it is not only famous for electronics; it has also become famous worldwide as being a gathering place for *otaku* (roughly, "geeky nerds"). It is also known as Otaku Town. This transformation came about after Akihabara had become full of computer and software shops.

In the latter half of the 1990s, video games featuring *bishōjo* (pretty underage girls) made their appearance, and stores dealing in this software or related goods became quite popular. Recently, Akihabara has become known as a center of *bishōjo* culture and its goods, which are quite unrelated to electronics.

Qなぜ、神田神保町には古書店がこんなに多いのですか？

東京の神田神保町は「世界最大の書店街」となっていて、多くの古書店が軒を連ねているだけではなく、大型書店や出版社、出版問屋なども点在しています。これは、1913年に2000戸以上が焼失する大きな火事があり、その焼け跡につくられた古書店が人気を博したことから、書店が増えだしたことに起因しています。この周辺には、大学や専門学校などが多く「学生街」が形成されていたことも大きな要因だったのでしょう。

神田神保町は、楽器店やスポーツ用品店、安価な飲食店が多いことでも有名ですが、世界的にもこうした傾向が見られる街はいくつかあり、パリのカルチェ・ラタンなどと比較されます。

Qなぜ、芸者の姿があまり見られないのですか？

芸者（芸妓）は、酒席において、歌や踊りで興を添えて、客をもてなす職業であり、華美な着物を着て、化粧で顔を白くするのは、そのための定型的なスタイルです。芸者文化が隆盛をきわめたのは江戸時代のことで、現在は、その文化を残そうとしている一部地域に限って、こうした職業が残されているだけになっています。

京都の祇園に行けばその姿を見ることができますが、それ以外の町では芸者はいても数が少なく、あまり見られません。在日外国人の間の有名なジョークに、「芸者を３回見たら、あなたは日本に長くいすぎた」というものがあるくらいで、フジヤマやシンカンセンは見られてもゲイシャはなかなか見られないのです。

■ Why are there so many used-book stores in the Kanda Jimbōchō district?

The Kanda Jimbōchō district in Tokyo is the world's largest used-book center. But in addition to the huge number of used-book stores, the area also has a good number of super bookstores, publishers, wholesalers, and other related businesses. It all started in 1913 when a fire destroyed over 2,000 houses in the area. A used-book store set up shop in the ruins, and due to its popularity, other used-book stores followed its lead. The fact that there are a good number of universities and vocational schools in the district, which create a university town atmosphere, is also a big factor.

Kanda Jimbōchō is also known for its musical instrument stores and sporting goods shops and for its cheap eating and drinking establishments. There are a number of comparable districts throughout the world, such as the Latin Quarter in Paris.

■ Why is it that you rarely see a geisha?

A geisha (or *geigi*) is a professional entertainer whose job is to entertain guests and add zest to a party through song and dance. They dress in beautiful kimonos and apply traditional heavy, white makeup. Geisha culture reached its peak in the Edo period (1600-1868), but today it survives in only a few places that have made an effort to preserve it.

You can see geishas if you go to the Gion district in Kyoto, but in other cities there are so few of them that you are not likely to be so lucky. A joke among foreigners living in Japan goes like this: "If you've seen a geisha three times, you've been in Japan too long." Of the three symbols of Japan in foreign eyes—Fujiyama, geisha, and the shinkansen—Mt. Fuji and the shinkansen are not hard to find, but geisha have become next to impossible to spot.

なぜ、Q クルマが走っていなくても赤信号で止まるのですか？

海外では、クルマが通行していない場合には赤信号でも横断歩道を渡る歩行者が多いのに対して、日本では赤信号のときにはどんな状況でも信号が変わるのを待つ人がほとんどです。

これは幼少時からそのように教育されているからだと言えるでしょう。警察にしても、歩行者の信号無視に対して取り締まりまではしなくても、注意をするのが通常です。こうした背景には、決められたルールを尊重する生真面目な性格があるのでしょう。とかくせっかちで急ぎがちな日本人ですから、こんなところで「ゆったり」を味わうのもいいかもしれません。

なぜ、Q クルマは左側を走るのですか？

アメリカやヨーロッパの多くの国では、クルマは右側通行になっているのに対して、日本やイギリス、オーストラリアなどではクルマは左側通行になっています。

なぜ、そうなったかについては諸説ありますが、かつての日本では、左腰に刀を差していた侍が道の左側を歩いていたため、すれ違う際に刀がぶつかってトラブルにならないようにカゴや荷馬車も左側を通るようにしていたのが、この習慣の始まりだとも言われています。

イギリスも日本と同じように左腰に剣を携えていた騎士たちが左側を歩いていたことからこの習慣が生まれ、アメリカでは御者が左側に座ることが多かった馬車が右側を通っていたことから逆になったと伝えられています。

なお、日本では1900年に人もクルマも左側通行をするように決められましたが、1950年に、クルマは左側通行で歩行者は右側通行と決め直されています。

■ Why do pedestrians stop for red lights even when there is no traffic?

Outside of Japan it is not unusual to see pedestrians cross the street against a red light when no cars are coming. In contrast, Japanese almost always wait for the light to change before crossing, no matter what the traffic is like.

This is undoubtedly due to training from an early age. As for the police, they are not likely to charge anyone with a crime, but they will usually give a warning. This phenomenon shows the serious side of the Japanese character, the one that adheres to the rules. Japanese are usually in a rush to get somewhere, so this may be a good time for them to "take it easy."

■ Why do cars travel on the left side of the road?

In the United States and many countries in Europe, cars travel on the right side of the road. In Japan, Great Britain, and Australia, however, they travel on the left.

There are a number of theories as to how this came about. In Japan, the custom is said to start with the fact that samurai wore their swords on their left hip, and to make sure that no one bumped into their sword, which would amount to an insult and lead to trouble, they walked on the left side of the road. This led to palanquins and horse-drawn wagons also keeping to the left.

In Great Britain, the origin of this custom is said to be somewhat the same, with sword-carrying knights traveling on left side of the road. In the United States, it is said that drivers usually sat on the left side of their carriages, which lead to the carriages traveling on the right.

In 1900 it was actually decided in Japan that both vehicles and pedestrians would keep to the left, but in 1950 that was changed so that while cars kept to the left, pedestrians stayed on the right.

なぜ、Q ■クルマをぴかぴかに磨くのですか？

ほこりだらけ、キズだらけのクルマが走っている様子は世界各地で見かけられますが、日本では洗車を欠かさず、常にキレイにしているドライバーが大半です。これは、キレイ好きな性格もあるのでしょうが、クルマに対する意識のあらわれともいえます。日本人のなかには、クルマを単なる移動の道具とは考えず、もっとも大切な所有物と見ている人も多いのです。

住宅事情が悪いこととも関係あるのでしょうが、クルマの中がもっともリラックスできる空間だと感じている人も珍しくはありません。そのため、車の中にカーペットを敷いて土足禁止にしたり、シャンデリアを吊るすなどして生活空間に近づける人もいるほどです。

夜間に光るナンバープレートなどを付けて、外装部分でも飾り立てようと努力している人も少なくありません。

なぜ、Q 駅のアナウンスはあんなにうるさいのですか？

電車の目的地や発車時間、到着するホームなどをアナウンスするのは普通のことですが、日本の駅では、過剰サービスともいえるような説明や注意がなされている場合がよくあります。「白線の内側をお歩きください」「忘れ物のないようにご注意ください」「降りる方が先となります」といった当然のことまで、何度もアナウンスされるケースが珍しくないのです。

親切心とも言えるのでしょうが、少しうがった見方をすれば、責任回避の姿勢だとも捉えられます。つまり、何かの事故やトラブルが起きたとき、駅側としては「事前に注意を促していた」と弁明することができるからです。

世界には発車のベルもアナウンスもないままに列車が出発する国もあれば、1、2時間遅れても普通と思って

■ Why do Japanese spend so much time keeping their cars clean?

All over the world you can see dirty, scratched-up cars on the roads, but in Japan the majority of drivers keep their cars washed and sparkling clean. This may be partly due to the fact that Japanese have a fetish for keeping things clean, but it may also have something to do with their attitude toward their cars. Many Japanese think of their car not just as a tool for getting from one place to another, but as a precious possession.

This may have something to do with the poor housing situation in Japan, but in any case there are a good many people who feel that their car is the place where they can best sit back and relax. There are even people who put in carpeting, have passengers remove their shoes, and even hang chandeliers. They are making the car as livable a space as they possibly can.

There are quite a few people who also spend time on decorating the exterior of their car, putting on license plates that glow in the dark and whatnot.

■ Why are there so many announcements at train stations?

While there is nothing odd about announcing destinations, departure times, and arrival platforms, it can't be denied that many explanations and warnings at Japanese train stations are excessive. "Walk inside the white line." "Be careful not to leave anything behind." "People getting off the train have priority." It is not unusual to hear repeated announcements like this, including things that could just as well be left to common sense.

You could say that they are just being especially considerate. But to take a harsher view of the matter, you could say that it is all an attempt to avoid responsibility. In other words, if there is an accident or trouble of some kind, the station can always say that they issued a warning.

There are some countries where trains depart without a warning

いる国もあります。そんな中で、「到着が３分遅れ、たいへんご迷惑をおかけしました」などということまで何度も繰り返してアナウンスするのは、お国ぶりのひとつなんでしょうか？

Qなぜ、電車の中で眠れるのですか？

スーツ姿の男性や女性が電車の中で警戒心を持たずに眠っている姿を目にすると、外国の人は驚くようです。日本ではお馴染みの光景にもなっていますが、これも仕方がない部分はあるのでしょう。

東京などでは、オフィスが集中している都心部ほど家賃が高くなるため、都心から離れた場所に住居を求めて、１時間ほどの時間をかけて通勤する人が少なくありません。なかには、片道２時間をかけての通勤をしている人もいるくらいです。ただでさえ働きすぎと言われている日本人が通勤にこれだけ時間をかけていれば、慢性的な睡眠不足になってしまうのも無理はないでしょう。

それにしても、こんなに安心して眠れるのは治安がいい証拠だとも言え、自慢していいことなのかもしれません。

bell or even an announcement. There are others where a one or two hour delay is taken as being normal. In good old Japan, however, you get repeated announcements saying, "The train will be three minutes late in arriving. Sorry for the inconvenience." Is there something typically Japanese about this?

■ Why is it that Japanese can sleep so soundly on the train?

In the eyes of foreign visitors to Japan, it is apparently a little surprising to see women and men in suits sleeping soundly on the train, as if they didn't have a worry in the world. Japanese are so used to this scene that they don't even think about it, but there is, I believe, a good explanation.

Because the closer you get to the business center of a big city like Tokyo, the higher the rent is, many people live in the suburbs. As a result, it is not unusual for them to spend a hour commuting to work. There are even some people who take two hours, one way. Given that Japanese are often criticized for overworking anyway, it stands to reason that if they spend this much time commuting, they are bound to end up being chronically sleep-deprived.

Still, to be able to sleep so soundly, without feeling the least bit insecure, must be due to reliable public safety. In that sense, it is something to brag about, I suppose.

12 テレビ

なぜ、Q

「韓流ブーム」なのですか？

「韓流」とは韓国大衆文化を指す言葉で、2000年頃に台湾で韓国ドラマのブームが起きたことから、この言葉が生まれました。日本では、少し遅れて2003年に、韓国で制作されたドラマ『冬のソナタ』が放送されたことから爆発的なブームが起きています。

この要因はいろいろ分析されていますが、よく指摘されるのは、『冬のソナタ』のストーリーは、1970年代から80年代に日本でつくられていたドラマに似ていて、懐かしさとともに共感を生んだのではないかということです。要するに、日本のドラマがある種、洗練化されてきているなかで、少し古くさいともいえる恋愛ドラマがかえって新鮮に捉えられたというわけです。

このブームを盛り上げたのは主に中高年女性層でしたが、彼女たちが韓国人俳優をアイドル視して、「追っかけ」をしたことは社会現象にもなりました。この現象については、主婦などが擬似恋愛的に熱狂する対象として、日本人では身近すぎるし、欧米人では現実味がなさすぎるのに対して、韓国人の場合はちょうどいい距離感が見出せたのではないか、と指摘する声もあります。

なぜ、Q

「紅白歌合戦」は「青白」ではないのですか？

たしかに対抗するものを「東西対抗」というように、正反対のものを表現したいのなら、「アジアの常識」からいって「青白」の方がピッタリでしょう。

■ Why has there been such a boom of Korean pop culture in Japan?

Actually, the craze for Korean pop culture first started in Taiwan in 2000 with Korean movie dramas. It was at this time that the name of the craze (Kanryū, or Korean Wave) was created. It wasn't until 2003, starting with the broadcast of the Korean-made TV drama "Winter Sonata," that the Kanryū boom exploded onto the Japanese scene.

Many reasons have been given for the boom. One of the more prevalent is that the story line of "Winter Sonata" is similar to dramas made in Japan from the 1970s and 1980s, creating a sense of nostalgia and shared experience. In other words, recent Japanese dramas have attained a certain level of refinement, and by contrast this somewhat old-fashioned romance seemed new and fresh.

The driving force behind this boom consisted mainly of middle-aged women, who created a social phenomenon by not only idolizing the actors but also becoming their groupies. As to how Korean actors should become the object of these housewives' feelings of passionate pseudo-love, it has been pointed out that Japanese actors wouldn't do because they were too familiar; Westerners wouldn't do because they lacked reality; Koreans stood at exactly the right point between too near and too distant.

■ Why is it the "Red and White Song Battle" instead of the "Blue and White Song Battle"?

It's true that, from an Asian perspective, if you want to express opposition (as in "East-West rivalry"), it should be "blue and white."

というのは、もともと東西南北には東→青、西→白、南→赤（朱)、北→黒（玄）という色がわりふられているのです。この考え方からすれば、歌手が紅組と白組に分かれて対抗するというＮＨＫの歳末人気番組、「紅白歌合戦」は「青白」といった方がふさわしいでしょう。

これは４つの方角が、東は青龍、西は白虎、南は朱雀、北は玄武という四神に護られているという考えから出てきたものです。高松塚古墳やキトラ古墳の壁にこの四神が描かれていたのもその一例です。

この「常識」はアジア全体に広く浸透していて、黒海とか紅海というのも、北の海、南の海という意味で、水の色ではありません。

また方角には四季もわりふられていて、東→春、西→秋、南→夏、北→冬となっています。ここから青春、白秋、朱夏、玄冬といった言葉が出てきています。

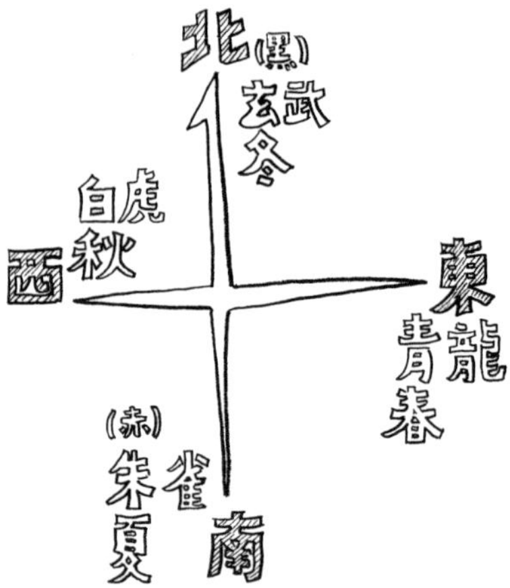

ただ「紅白」は源氏の白と平家の赤といった歴史的な伝統もあるうえに、めでたいときに使われる色ですから、歌合戦といった華やかなものにはピッタリのものなのでしょう。

なぜ、Q ワイドショーがこんなに流行っているのですか？

ワイドショーとは和製英語で、放送時間が長く、幅広いテーマを扱うことからこの名がついたものです。情報番組の一種ですが、生放送であることを基本として、ニュースや芸能情報、生活情報などを扱います。ただし、ニュースを扱う際にも、一般の報道番組とは違って、政

In Asia, the four directions have been assigned colors: east is blue (azure); west, white; south, red (vermillion); and north, black. Given this, "blue and white" would express exactly the element of rivalry in the year-end NHK music show, "Red and White Song Battle," in which popular singers are divided up into two competing sides labeled red and white.

These colors come from the idea that four mythological creatures are guarding the four directions: a blue (azure) dragon is guarding the east; a white tiger the west; a red (vermillion) bird the south; and a black tortoise the north. This can be seen on the walls of the seventh-century Takamatsuzuka and Kitora Tombs.

This thinking is accepted as a matter of course in Asia, and so when a "black sea" or a "red sea" is mentioned, the reference is to "north" and "south," not to the color of the water.

Taking this one step further, the four directions are also assigned a season: east is spring; west, autumn; south, summer; and north, winter. Then combing the colors assigned to the directions with the seasons, we get alternative poetic ways of referring to the seasons. The four seasons become blue (azure) spring, red (vermillion) summer, white autumn, and black winter.

In the case of the "Red and White Song Battle," however, there is another tradition in Japan that associates the colors white and red with the two powerful warrior clans that fought for power in the twelfth century, the Minamoto (Genji = white) and Taira (Heike = red). Since red and white are also used to mark happy occasions, the colors red and while seem perfect for a colorful music show like the "Red and White Song Battle."

■ Why are "wide shows" so popular?

The phrase "wide show" was coined in Japan—that is, it is Japanese English—and it refers to the fact that the TV shows in question are long and deal with a "wide" variety of subject matter. They are news and information programs, usually live, and deal with the general news, celebrity news, and tips and news about

治・経済の話題よりも殺人事件などを扱うことが多く、加害者や被害者の私生活面を追うなどして、「いかに、視聴者の感情に訴えるか」が重視されています。

視聴者の中心は主婦で、家の中での空いた時間に提供する娯楽という意味合いが強く、主婦同士の会話に話題を提供する役割も果たしているわけです。

日本初のワイドショーは、1964年に放送開始された『モーニングショー』だとされていますが、この番組はアメリカの『トゥデイ』をモデルにして作られたといいます。アメリカのソープオペラに似た番組としては「昼ドラ」と呼ばれる浮気をテーマにした連続ドラマがありますが、ワイドショーにしても、その狙いはソープオペラと大差がないと言えるでしょう。

なぜ、Q アイドルと呼ばれる人たちがもてはやされるのですか？

アイドルとは本来、「崇拝される神の偶像」という意味なのですが、日本では「子供や若者に人気がある歌手やタレント」を指す言葉としてのみ定着しています。とくに、1970年代から80年代にかけては、テレビの歌番組が高視聴率を取っていたため、アイドルの全盛期になっていました。人気の高いアイドルが一般人よりもヘタな歌をヒットさせていたのもこの頃です。

ただ、歌番組の人気にかげりが出てくると、アイドルもさまざまなジャンルに分化してきました。音楽活動を中心とするアイドルも残りましたが、そのほかには、写真集や雑誌などのモデルとして活躍するグラビア・アイドルや、お笑い番組を中心に活躍するバラドル（バラエティ番組のアイドルの略称）などが登場しました。

複数のタレントが出演するバラエティ番組が非常に多いこともあって、こうしたアイドルたちは毎日テレビに出演しています。

everyday life. But even when they deal with the general news, they do it differently from standard news programs. Rather than politics and the economy, they are more likely to cover murders and other crimes, and probe into the lives of the victims and perpetrators. The emphasis is on how successfully they can appeal to the viewers' emotions.

Wide show viewers consist mostly of housewives, and the programs provide a bit of entertainment in between housework. They also provide topics of conversation when housewives gather to talk.

The first "wide show" made its appearance in 1964 and was called "The Morning Show." It is said to have been modeled on the American program the "Today" show. Another program, which is similar to an American soap opera, is literally called a "noon drama" and is a series of programs that deal with infidelities and love affairs. The audience that the wide shows cultivate is not much different from that of the "noon dramas."

■ Why are so-called pop idols made so much of?

The original meaning of "idol" is a picture or sculpture of a god that is used for worship. In Japan, however, only the secondary meaning of the word is used, that is, "a singer or entertainer who is popular among children and young people." Particularly in the 1970s to the 1980s, TV singing shows got such high ratings that this period is consider the high point for singer idols. It was around this time that singers who were no better than amateurs managed to produce hit songs.

Later, however, the singing shows lost popularity, and the singer idols got work in various other fields. Some of these idols continued to work mainly with music, of course, but many moved into new areas—such as working as models for photo albums and magazines, or appearing on comedy-variety shows.

Since many of these variety shows feature a number of entertainers, these idols end up appearing on TV almost daily.

なぜ、Q タレントが政治問題について発言するのですか？

ワイドショーでは、政治問題や事件について評論するコメンテーターが存在していますが、近年は専門家に限らず、スポーツ選手やお笑いタレントなどの著名人がコメンテーターに起用されるケースが増えています。

また、ワイドショーに限らず、お笑いタレントなどが政治問題を中心に扱う番組の司会をするケースも見られます。これは、専門家が難しい解説をするよりも、視聴者にとって親しみやすい存在がわかりやすく解説したほうが、「番組が身近なものになって、視聴率を上げやすい」と考えられているためなのでしょう。

日本には政治に関心を持たない若い人が多いのですが、こうした番組によって、その傾向が改善されてきていると言えるのかもしれません。

なぜ、Q アメリカの大スターたちがコマーシャルに出ているのですか？

アメリカから来た人たちは、メグ・ライアン、レオナルド・ディカプリオといったハリウッドの大俳優たちが日本のコマーシャルに出ているのを見てビックリします。欧米では、大俳優が商品の宣伝をすることは「はしたない」ことであり、特別なことでもない限りコマーシャルに出ることはほとんどありません。

また、コマーシャルの作り方が違うということも原因として大きいのでしょう。欧米のコマーシャルは、その商品がいかにいいものであるかということを説明するために全力をそそぎますが、日本ではどんな俳優やタレントがその商品をすすめるかということに重点をおいているからです。

■ Why do entertainers speak up about political problems?

On morning "wide shows," there is usually a professional commentator who analyzes political problems and events, but recently there seems to have been an increase in the number of cases where someone else, or several other people, play that role. This person may be a specialist in some field, but he or she may also be a sports celebrity or a well-known comedian.

And this is not confined just to wide shows. There are also instances of a comedian or some such entertainer acting as the host on a program focusing on politics. The reasoning behind this is that it is easier to raise the program's ratings if, rather than the difficult commentary of a specialist, the host is someone who is well-known to the audience and can give commentary that is easy to understand.

Many young Japanese have no interest in politics, but thanks to programs like this, the situation may be improving somewhat.

■ Why do top American movie stars appear in Japanese commercials?

When people visiting Japan from the United States see top stars like Meg Ryan or Leonardo DiCaprio appearing in Japanese commercials, they are more than a little surprised. In Europe and the United States, it is "uncool" for big stars to appear in commercials, and unless there are special circumstances, they very rarely do.

Another factor may be the way the commercials are made. In the West, the point of the commercial is to explain how wonderful the product is; in Japan, it is to show off the stars who are promoting the product.

13 スポーツ

なぜ、野球が盛んで、強いのですか？

世界的にメジャーな競技といえば、サッカーが挙げられますが、日本ではサッカーよりも先に野球が国民に広がりました。日本サッカー協会の前身が創立されたのは1921年のことですが、野球では1903年に早慶戦（早稲田大学と慶応大学の対抗戦）がスタートしています。

そして、1925年に東京六大学野球が始まり、野球観戦がレジャーとして定着しました。また、プロ野球の公式戦が始まったのが1936年であるのに対して、プロサッカーは1993年に始まったばかりというように、歴史の違いは明らかです。そうした背景があるからこそ、野球は国民的スポーツとして浸透したわけです。

2006年のワールド・ベースボール・クラシックでも優勝したように、日本の野球のレベルはたしかに高いと言えるでしょう。ヨーロッパなどでは野球はそれほど普及していないうえ、アジアにおいても他国より半世紀近く早くプロ野球が発足していたのですから、優秀な選手が生まれやすい土壌にあるのは当然かもしれません。

なぜ、巨人ファンが多いのですか？

大日本東京野球倶楽部を前身とする巨人は、現存する日本最古のプロ野球球団です。1934年に行われた日米対抗野球の全日本チームのメンバーが主体となって結成され、1936年から開始されたプロリーグには東京巨人軍と改称して参加し、優勝を果たしています。プロ野球

■ Why is baseball so popular in Japan, and why are Japanese so good at it?

If you were asked to name the world's top competitive sport, you would have to say soccer, I suppose. But in Japan, baseball attracted a wide following much earlier than soccer. The predecessor to the present Japan Football Association was formed in 1921, whereas the first baseball game in the famous rivalry between Waseda and Keio universities was played in 1903.

In 1925 the collegiate Tokyo Big 6 Baseball League got under way, and baseball became established as a spectator sport. Furthermore, whereas the first professional baseball game was played in 1936, professional soccer didn't get started until 1993. The historical difference between the two sports is clear. Given this background, it is understandable that baseball should become the national sport.

The level of baseball in Japan is, without a doubt, rather high, as can be seen from Japan winning the 2006 World Baseball Classic. Baseball is not played much in Europe, and in Asia Japan has almost a fifty-year head start in setting up a professional league. So perhaps Japan simply provides the fertile soil necessary for raising talented players.

■ Why are there so many Giants fans?

The Giants (originally the Great Japan Tokyo Baseball Club) is the oldest professional Japanese baseball team in existence. Many of its original members came from the all-star team that played a touring American team in 1934. Renamed the Tokyo Giants, it took part in the first professional season in 1936 and won the pennant. Since the

発足当初から最強のチームであった巨人には、必然的にスターが集まるため、これが人気の要因のひとつになっています。

もうひとつ、このチームを発足させたのが、正力松太郎という人物だったことも大きな意味を持っています。正力氏は、日本最大級の発行部数を誇る『読売新聞』の当時のオーナーだったからです。その後テレビ放送が開始されると、系列局である日本テレビが優先的に全国放送をして、さらに高い認知度を獲得していきました。地元にプロ球団を持たない地域の人々が巨人ファンになっていったのも、当然のなりゆきでした。

ただし、価値観の多様化やテレビの多チャンネル化が進む現在では、他チームのファンが増加している傾向にあります。

なぜ、Q 日本のスポーツには格闘技が多いのですか？

さまざまなルーツを持つ格闘技は世界中に存在していますが、日本における格闘技の多くは、その発祥の歴史を遡れば、「武術」に行き着きます。つまり、武士が戦闘のため、あるいは護身のために体得した技術です。

明治以降は、それらが義務教育にも取り入れられるようになりました。もともとは武士階級の修練技術であり、殺人技術だったものが、一般的な精神修養の手段として、あるいはスポーツ競技として発展していったわけです。

なぜ、Q 日本のスポーツは「道」になるのですか？

スポーツの語源は「disport」だといわれていて、その意味は「気晴らし」「楽しみ」「遊ぶ」になります。本来、スポーツの概念とは、そういうものだったわけです。日本において、この言葉が広まったのは大正時代（1912-1926）の末期です。ただし、この当時、スポー

Giants were the strongest team from the very start, it naturally attracted more star players to the team. This is one reason for its huge popularity.

Another very important factor is that the person responsible for establishing the team was Matsutarō Shōriki. At the time, he was the owner of Japan's largest newspaper, the *Yomiuri*. Then, when TV began telecasting baseball games, the broadcast rights were given to a station related to the newspaper, Nihon Television, and this raised awareness of the team even higher. It was only natural that in regions that didn't have a professional team, everyone became Giants fans.

However, with the present diversification of interests and the increased number of television channels, the number of fans loyal to other teams is on the rise.

■ Why are most Japanese sports martial arts?

Martial arts exist throughout the world with various roots, but if you trace back the origin of most Japanese martial arts, you come to bujutsu ("the arts of the samurai"). That is, you come to the arts or techniques learned by samurai to protect themselves or to use in battle.

After the start of the Meiji period (1868-1912), most of these arts were incorporated into compulsory education. What was originally a form of mental and physical training for the samurai class, as well as a means of killing people, evolved into a form of character building or into a sport to be enjoyed by everyone.

■ Why are Japanese martial arts referred to as a "way of life"?

The English word "sports" is said to come from the word "disport," which means to have a good time, to enjoy oneself, to play. This, after all, is the original concept behind Western sports. The word itself first became widely used in Japan at the end of the Taishō

ツという言葉は、欧米から輸入された野球などの競技を指すものとして使われていました。つまり、当時の日本ではスポーツと武道は分けられていて、武道とはあくまで自己を高める目的で、「道を究める精神」や「あるべき理想」を追求する方法と考えられていたわけです。

こういう理由で、競技名の末尾に「道」という文字がついているのです。ですから野球でも、ボールとバットで遊ぶゲームということではなく、これを通して精神を養うものとしたいのであれば「野球道」ということになります。

この精神性が海外では現在でも非常に高い評価を受けています。武道に関連した英文書はロングセラーとなっていて、柔道の嘉納治五郎、合気道の植芝盛平などはほとんど「信仰」といってもいいような尊敬の対象となっています。

Qなぜ、相撲は日本の国技なのですか？

相撲の起源は、４世紀ごろに、野見宿禰が当麻蹴速を蹴り殺した対戦にあるとされていて、このことは古代の史書『日本書紀』にも描かれています。日本最古の書『古事記』にも相撲の記述は見つかるように、古い歴史をもつ競技です。

聖武天皇が相撲を観覧するなど、奈良（710-794）・平安時代（794-1185）から相撲は宮中の行事であり、娯楽だったのです。また、鎌倉幕府を開いた源頼朝（1147-1199）や、戦国時代を統一に導いた織田信長（1534-1582）といった時の権力者も相撲を奨励しました。とくに信長は、現在の土俵の原型を考案したとも言われています。

このように、日本の象徴である天皇家や権力者が、相撲を隆盛させた歴史があります。また、現在でも神社には土俵が設置されていることがあるように、一般的には相撲が神事になっていました。こうした背景から、相撲を国技とする拠り所が成立していたわけです。

period (1912-1926). At that time, however, the word was used only in reference to Western sports like baseball. A distinction was made between sports and budō (or martial arts). Budō was strictly seen as a way to make oneself into a better person, a way of probing into the order of things, a way of finding out how life should be lived.

This is indicated by the inclusion of the suffix *dō* in the word, which means "way" or "path." If you want to refer to baseball (*yakyū*) as this kind of spiritual path or way, rather than just a game played with a ball and bat, you can add *dō* to the word, producing *yakyūdō* ("the way of baseball").

This spiritual side of Japanese martial arts is seen by the outside world as a very positive thing. Many English books on budō have become long-sellers. And the founders of Judo, Jigorō Kanō, and Aikido, Morihei Ueshiba, are respected to the point of idolization.

■ Why is Sumo considered the national sport?

The origins of Sumo apparently go back to about 400 AD when Nomi no Sukune defeated, and kicked to death, Taima no Kehaya. This is recorded in the second oldest Japanese historical document, *The Chronicles of Japan* (720). Sumo is also mentioned in Japanese oldest book, *Records of Ancient Matters* (680).

We can conclude from this that Sumo's history goes back over 2,000 years. We know that Emperor Shōmu (701-756) attended a Sumo tournament, and that Sumo was a form of recreation in court life in the Nara (710-794) and Heian (794-1185) periods. We also know that the founder of the Kamakura shogunate, Minamoto Yoritomo (1147-1199), as well as the unifier of the country during the Warring States period, Oda Nobunaga (1534-1582), were both supporters of Sumo, in addition to other powerful figures of various periods. It is even said that Oda Nobunaga proposed the prototype of the present-day Sumo ring.

History therefore shows us that both emperors and some of Japan's greatest leaders have contributed to Sumo's popularity. Back then,

ただし、「国技」というのは法律で決まっているのではなく、1909年に相撲のための会館ができたときに「国技館」と名付けたので、「相撲は国技」というイメージができあがったのです。名前は大切ですね。

なぜ、Q 大相撲に外国人力士が多いのですか？

価値観の多様化によって、資質のある日本の少年たちが他競技に目を向けてしまい、力士を志す日本人が減少していることが、その背景にあるのでしょう。そこで、才能のある人間を発掘するために海外にも目を向けるようになったわけです。もともと肉体的パワーにおいては、外国人、とくに欧米人は体が大きいのですから、相撲のような格闘技においてはアドバンテージがあるわけです。

近年、相撲の認知度が世界に広まり、外国人力士の活躍が伝えられていることにより、外国人にとっても相撲が馴染みやすい存在になっています。その先駆け的存在といえる小錦は「人種差別によって横綱になれなかった」と発言して話題を呼びました。その正否はともかくとして、その後に外国人横綱が誕生したことでも、外国人にとっての相撲はさらに身近な存在になったと言えるのでしょう。

とくに、もともと相撲に似た競技が国内にあるモンゴルからは、高い才能を持つ力士が次々と日本に来て、上位の番付を席巻しています。また、ヨーロッパ出身で、アマレス経験のある巨体の力士などもその力を発揮しているため、日本の力士が劣勢になっているのが大相撲の現状です。

Sumo was also generally considered a religious rite, as shown by the fact that Sumo rings are found within the grounds of Shintō shrines. From all this, we can see that there was sufficient reason to make Sumo the national sport.

However, Sumo is not *legally* the national sport. When in 1909 a new arena was built for Sumo, it was called the National Sports Arena, which strongly implied that Sumo was the national sport. Names are quite important, it seems.

■ Why are there so many foreign Sumo wrestlers?

The underlying reason is probably that sports have diversified, and the number of talented young Japanese wanting to become Sumo wrestlers has declined. To fill this gap, an effort has been made to find promising talent abroad. In terms of physical strength, foreigner wrestlers (in particular Americans and Europeans) are larger than Japanese and have a definite advantage in a combat sport like Sumo.

Recently, Sumo has become more widely known abroad, and as the performance of foreign wrestlers is taken up by overseas media, foreigners no longer feel that Sumo is somehow alien. One of the first foreign wrestlers, Konishiki, apparently said that he couldn't become a yokozuna because of prejudice against foreigners. Whether that's true or not, a foreigner did become a yokozuka after that, so foreigners now undoubtedly feel that Sumo is something even closer and more friendly.

In recent years, many talented wrestlers have been coming from Mongolia, where they practice a form of wrestling that is very similar to Sumo. In fact, Mongolian wrestlers now dominate the upper ranks. In addition, huge European wrestlers with amateur wrestling experience are also performing well. That, in short, is the present situation, with Japanese wrestlers fighting an uphill battle.

14 会社

なぜ、日本人はこんなに働くのですか？

実をいうと、日本人はもともと勤勉だったわけではありません。古い海外の文献ではむしろ、怠惰な姿が描かれていることもあるくらいです。実際、江戸時代以前の日本人は、夏場などには涼しい午前中しか働かなかったと言います。

そんな日本人が勤勉になったターニングポイントはふたつあると言われています。明治時代の富国強兵政策のもとに、産業や軍事の面で西洋に追いつこうとしたとき。それから、戦後の廃墟から復興しようと国民全体が一丸となってがんばった高度経済成長期です。

日本人は、個よりも集団を重んじる風潮があるため、国を挙げての政策が掲げられたり、戦後復興のために皆が頑張る風潮が出てきた中で、勤勉こそが美徳と信じ込んでいったのでしょう。つまり、まず集団として勤勉であるべきとの価値観が生まれ、個人としてもそれに従うようになったというわけです。そこで生じた新たな性格が、日本人のDNAに刷り込まれているとも言えるのかもしれません。

なぜ、「根回し」が必要なのですか

日本人は、議論が苦手な民族と言われています。イエス・ノーをはっきり言わず、曖昧なままにしておくことが多いのも、物事に白黒をつけることを好まないからだと言えるでしょう。何かを決定しようとするとき、意見

Company Life

■ Why are Japanese such hard workers?

The truth is, Japanese weren't always hard workers. When you look at historical accounts of the Japanese people written by non-Japanese, Japanese are even described as being lazy. For instance, it is said that before the Edo period (1600-1868) Japanese only worked in the cool of the morning during summertime.

There are perhaps two major turning points that resulted in Japanese becoming hard workers. One was government policy in the Meiji period (1868-1912), when the whole country was urged to work hard so that Japan could overtake the West in industrial wealth and military strength. The other was the period of rapid economic growth that took place after World War II, when the country made a collective effort to recover from the ruins of war.

Since Japanese are more group-oriented than individual-oriented, when a national policy calling for total commitment is announced, or when there is a mass movement to recover from a war, "hard work" becomes a widely accepted virtue of the highest order. In other words, hard work is first seen as a virtue for the group as a whole, and then the individual falls in with the thinking of the group. This value system became imprinted on the Japanese character.

■ Why do Japanese feel it necessary to settle problems behind the scenes?

Japanese are said to be bad at open debate and public discussion. They don't want to give a straight yes or no answer. They prefer to leave things a little vague, not a clearly defined black or white.

の対立が起きそうだと思ったら、「根回し」と呼ばれる下工作を行います。「根回し」とは庭師の用語で、木を別の場所に移植するとき、前もってその木の根の回りを掘って準備することをいいます。

まず会議の出席者に事前に会い、こちらの考えを伝えます。相手に反対意見があるときには説得し、あるいは相手の意見もいれた案に変更します。このようにして確執を生まずに結論を出そうとするのです。

1400年も前に聖徳太子が起草した『十七条憲法』の第1条にある「和をもって尊しとなす」の精神は、こうしたなかにも生きているのかもしれません。

ただそんな日本人にしても、「根回し」という言葉を、和の精神にのっとったいい意味を持つ言葉と考えているわけではありません。本来は正々堂々と議論すべき問題を、裏でコソコソと処理してしまうというイメージがあるからです。

Qなぜ、学歴が重視されるのですか？

就職や出世において、学歴が重視される風潮は、日本に限らず、世界各地で見られます。学歴社会は、先進国か発展途上国であるかを問わずに見られ、日本よりもアメリカのほうがこうした偏重は強いとの指摘もあるほどです。大卒者と高卒者以下との生涯年収の差を見ても、日本は比較的小さなほうだとされています。

高度な産業社会が形成されている場合や、形成されていく過程においては、「どのような教育を受けてきたか」が人材判断の基準になるのは仕方がないことかもしれません。ただし、学歴社会における判断基準では世界各地で傾向の違いが見られま

When a decision has to be made, and it seems that there might be a clash of opinion, the problem is first discussed behind the scenes. This is called *nemawashi*, which is a gardening term referring to the preparation of the roots of a tree prior to moving it to a new location.

First, you meet with the people who are to take part in the meeting and explain your thinking. If someone has a different opinion, you try to persuade them, or if that fails, you include their thinking in a new proposal.

In this way, you try to arrive at a conclusion without creating hard feelings. In the seventh century, Prince Shōtoku drew up a seventeen article constitution in which he wrote, "Value harmony and avoid conflict." Perhaps this spirit is still alive among the Japanese people today.

However, even the Japanese themselves don't consider *nemawashi* to be an excellent example of "harmony" in action. With *nemawashi*, after all, problems that should be discussed openly are taken care of behind the scenes.

■ Why is one's educational background considered so important?

With regard to employment and future promotion, the emphasis on educational background is not limited to Japan, but is a worldwide trend. This seems to be true for both industrially advanced countries and developing countries. Some even say that the emphasis on educational background is stronger in the United States than in Japan. The difference in lifetime income between university graduates and those graduating from high school or lower is relatively small in Japan.

For highly industrialized countries as well as for those countries that are in the process of industrialization, making educational background a basis for judging new employees may be unavoidable. Even for societies that emphasize educational background, however, each country seems to have its own basis for judgment. While many

す。大学院で博士課程まで修了しているかどうかが問われる国が多いのに対し、日本では修了課程はあまり重視されず、「どのレベルの大学を出ているか」が問われがちです。これは、日本の大学では、卒業よりも入学が難しいという風潮があるからです。

幼少時や10代の頃にいかに競争に勝ち抜けたかが生涯を左右する部分も大きいわけですから、そうした意味では厳しい社会だとは言えるでしょう。

Qなぜ、転職がキャリアダウンにつながるのですか？

終身雇用制とは、いったん企業に就職すれば、その企業で定年になるまで勤めあげるシステムです。日本では、バブル景気が崩壊する1990年代半ばまでこの「終身雇用制」が常識になっていました。大企業の社員が会社を移ることはほとんどなく、もし会社を変わるとすれば、それは当人に欠陥があったり、重大な過失をしたのだと考えられたのです。

現在では企業がリストラのために社員を解雇するようになったので、そうした考え方も少なくなってきていますが、まだ転職はポジティブには捉えられにくいのです。

また、日本人が転職する際には、キャリアアップよりも「自分のやりたい仕事」が重視されている場合が多く、「人間関係の不和」などが理由になっている場合もよくあります。そうしたことからも、転職＝キャリアアップという考え方自体が日本人には浸透しにくいわけです。崩れかけてはいても、やはり日本はまだ「終身雇用の国」なのでしょう。

Qなぜ、フリーターがこんなに増えたのですか？

フリーターとは、1987年に生まれた言葉で、アルバイトで生計を立てている人たちを指します。厚生労働省は15～34歳の人と定義していますが、現実としては34

countries are concerned with whether a person has earned a PhD, Japan is more concerned with the reputation of the university attended. The reason for this is that getting into Japanese universities is more difficult than graduating from them.

To a considerable degree, a person's life is shaped by how successful he or she was in competing with other students in childhood and the teen years. In that sense, Japanese society can be said to be a tough place to grow up.

■ Why is changing jobs seen as a bad career move?

Lifetime employment means that once you join a firm, you stay there until retirement. This system was taken for granted in Japan until the end of the economic bubble in the mid 1990s. Employees at large firms rarely changed companies, and if they did, it was generally thought that something was wrong with them, or that they had made a huge mistake in their job.

Nowadays, with companies letting employees go as part of restructuring, this type of thinking is not as prevalent as it used to be, but nevertheless changing jobs is still not seen in a positive light.

When Japanese change companies, it is usually not to improve their career but to do the type of work that they really want to do. Personal relations is another reason that is often given. Thus for Japanese, a change in companies does not necessarily equal a positive career move. Even though lifetime employment is gradually breaking down, Japan is still dominated by its presence.

■ Why has the number of part-timers increased so much?

"Part-timer" is used here as a translation for the Japanese word *furītā*. This word was coined in 1987 to refer to people who made a living by doing part-time work. As defined by the Health, Labor and

歳以上の人も存在しています。87年前後の日本は好況にあり、深夜営業店舗の増大などから、非正社員の需要が高まっていました。こうした風潮により、アルバイトでも十分生活が成り立つようになり、最低限の生活費だけを得て、音楽や芸術の道を志しているような人たちにとっては追い風となりました。こうしてフリーターは一気に増加したのです。

ところが、90年代に入って不況となると、今度は企業側が人件費抑制のため、正社員の採用を減少させることになりました。これによって、就職を希望してもかなわない人がフリーターになっていったのです。フリーターが正社員への昇格を希望しても、なかなか受け入れられず、フリーター人口はさらに拡大しています。好況で生まれ、不況でさらに増えたのがフリーターと言えるでしょう。

Q なぜ、「ニート」と呼ばれる人たちが増えているのですか？

ニートとは、ごく簡単にいうと、15～34歳の非就学・非労働者を指します。もともとはイギリスで生まれた概念ですが、そのイギリスも含めた諸外国でこの言葉はほとんど使われておらず、現在ではイギリスにおいても「日本における若年非労働者」と捉えられているようです。

ニートが日本で増えている最大の理由は、バブル崩壊以降の長い不況にあると言えるでしょう。就職難により過度な競争を強いられた人たちが、その精神的疲労により無気力になるケースが多かったからです。現在は景気が回復しつつあると言われ、雇用状況も好転しつつあります。

それでも、最悪の就職氷河期とされていた1998年に求職活動に失敗した世代はすでに30歳を迎えており、希望する職種への就職が難しい年齢になっていることから、高年齢層のニートはむしろ増加する傾向にあります。

Welfare Ministry, *furītā* fall between the ages of fifteen and thirty-four, but in actuality some are older. Around 1987 the Japanese economy was booming, and with more stores staying open until late at night, there was a strong demand for part-time workers. This meant that it was possible to make a living working part-time. That was good news for people who wanted to make a minimal living and spend the rest of their time on music or art. As a result, the number of *furītā* increased dramatically.

However, the economy turned down in the 1990s, and corporations cut back on the hiring of full-time employees in order to reduce labor costs. Consequently, people who wanted to be employed full-time, but couldn't, ended up becoming *furītā*. With no hope of full-time employment, the number of *furītā* continued to expand. So you could say that *furītā* came into being in good times and grew in number in bad times.

■ Why are NEETs on the increase?

In short, NEETs refers to people between the ages of fifteen and thirty-four who are out of school and unemployed. This was originally a British acronym ((**N**ot currently engaged in **E**mployment, **E**ducation, or **T**raining), but now it is not used much, either in Great Britain or in any country other than Japan. In Great Britain, the term NEET now refers to a young unemployed Japanese person.

The biggest reason that the number of NEETs increased in Japan is the long economic downturn following the burst of the economic bubble. During this period, many people became mentally exhausted from the hard competition to get a job.

Today, the economy is looking up, and employment conditions are better. Still, the generation that failed to find employment in 1998, the "ice age" of unemployment, is now approaching thirty. Since thirty is a difficult age at which to find employment in one's desired field, we can expect the NEET population not only to remain unemployed but to gradually grow older.

NEETs can survive without working because many of them are

就職しなくても生活が成り立つのは、両親に依存しているケースが多いからです。それが可能であるのは国全体が豊かである証明でもありますが、それに甘える若者が増えているという指摘もあります。

ニートと混同されやすいフリーターは、非正社員であっても就労しているため、ニートには分類されません。また、求職活動をしている者は失業者であり、やはりニートとは別の分類になります。

dependent on their parents. This is possible because the country as a whole is prosperous, and the young increasingly take advantage of this situation.

NEETs are often confused with *furītā*, but the latter is employed, even though not full-time. Even if they happen to be unemployed, *furītā* are still seeking work, and therefore not to be classified with NEETs.

15 産業

なぜ、Q

日本の電気製品は世界を席巻したのですか？

世界を席巻した日本の電気製品の代表例としては、ソニーが発売した携帯型ステレオカセットプレーヤー「ウォークマン」が挙げられます。ウォークマンはもちろん商品名ですが、和製英語であるため、1979年の発売当初は、欧米では別の商品名で発売されていました。ところが、日本でウォークマンを購入して自国に持ち帰る欧米人が増えたことからその名が世界に広まり、結局、多くの国でもウォークマンとして発売されることになりました。

このウォークマンは、当時のソニーの名誉会長・井深大氏が、出張時の機内で気軽に音楽を楽しめるようにするため、「録音機能はいらないから、ステレオ回路を入れた軽いものを作ってほしい」と望んだことから開発されたものでした。そんな発想をそのまま商品にしてしまえる高い技術力が日本のメーカーの強みです。

この技術力は、機能の優秀性や先進性を持つ商品開発に活かされるだけではなく、製品の「安定度」と「長寿度」にも存分に発揮されていると言えるでしょう。故障が少なく、長く使用できる。これこそが日本製品の最大の特徴であり、欧米などでも高く認められた要因でした。

ただし最近では、日本に限らず、中国や韓国、インドなど、他のアジア地域の技術力も急成長を見せています。

■ Why have Japanese electric appliances become so dominant?

The most well-known example of a Japanese electric appliance that achieved world dominance is the portable stereo cassette player produced by Sony, the Walkman. Since the brand name "Walkman" is what you might call Japanese English (that is, English made in Japan), when the Walkman first went on sale in the United States and Europe in 1979, it was sold under another name. As it happened, however, many Westerners bought Walkmans in Japan and took them home, and the "Walkman" name spread around the world. As a result, the Walkman came to be sold under that name in most countries.

At the time, the chairman of Sony, Masaru Ibuka, wanted an easy way to listen to music on the plane when on business trips. He said that he didn't need a recording function; he just wanted something light with a stereo circuit. The Walkman was the result. Moving from a simple idea to a finished product is a technological strength that Japanese manufacturers have.

This technological strength appears not only in the development of products having superior functions or advanced capabilities, but also in the products' reliability and durability. They don't break down; they're long-lasting. This is the most outstanding feature of Japanese products, and the reason they have been so successful in the West.

Recently, however, Japan has been joined by China, South Korea, India, and other Asian countries that are growing rapidly in technological expertise.

なぜ、Q 日本のクルマは世界を席巻したのですか？

日本の電気製品が世界を席巻したのと同じように、日本の自動車メーカーはその技術力において高い評価を受けています。とくに優れていると認められている点も、やはり電気製品と同じで、「安定度」と「長寿度」です。寒冷地や僻地、あるいは大都市の危険地帯などでの故障は、ドライバーの生命まで危険にさらすことになりますから、その故障の少なさが高く評価されたものと思われます。「TOYOTA」「HONDA」など、日本の自動車メーカーの名前は、もはや世界共通語になっているとも言えるでしょう。

とはいえ、すべての面で外国車より優秀というわけではなく、運転感覚や高速性能においてはヨーロッパ車に先んじられていると言われています。

なぜ、Q 小型の製品を作るのが得意なのですか？

日本人は手先が器用な民族です。また、単に器用なだけではなく、「細部にこだわる」特性を持っています。ひとつの商品を作るときには、実用性だけにとどまらず、耐久性や見た目の美しさなどにまでこだわっていくのが日本人です。それが性能の高さを実現させると同時に、細やかな神経を必要とする小型製品の製造に活かされているのでしょう。

それに加えて、日本人には、韓国の評論家・李御寧氏が指摘したような「縮み志向」があるのかもしれません。日本の代表的なお土産のひとつである「扇子」は、大昔、紙がまだ貴重品だったころに、メモ用に使っていた木簡を綴じて持ち運びやすくしたことが起源になっていて、これが日本から世界への最初の輸出品だったとも言われています。また、乾電池を発明したのは日本人であり、電卓を世界ではじめて商品化したのも日本のシャープという会社です。

■ Why have Japanese automobiles been so successful?

Just as with electronics makers, Japanese auto manufacturers have won high praise for their technological expertise. The areas in which they are considered particularly outstanding are the same as those for electronics goods—reliability and durability. Breakdowns in cold climates or in out-of-the-way places, or even in dangerous parts of a city, can put a driver at risk. For this reason, reliability is very important. It is only natural, perhaps, that names like Toyota and Honda should have become household words.

Still, Japanese automobiles are not superior to their competitors in every respect. European cars are a step ahead when it comes to ease of handling and high-speed capabilities.

■ Why are the Japanese good at making small things?

Japanese are good with their hands, but that is not all. Japanese also like to pay attention to detail. When making something, Japanese are not only interested in its practicality, but also with its durability and in its outward appearance. These Japanese characteristics not only make high-performance products possible, they are also good for manufacturing products that are small and compact.

As the Korean critic O-Young Lee says, perhaps Japanese are especially good at reducing things in size, to making them smaller, more compact. One favorite item for foreign visitors to take home with them is the Japanese folding fan (*sensu*). This fan, which consists of paper pasted over a frame of foldable ribs, has its roots over a thousand years in the past. Paper was expensive then, and memos were written on slats of wood. The prototype of the folding fan was created, it is said, when a number of these slats were bound together for easy portability. The folding fan was Japan's first export to the outside world. Japanese also invented the dry cell battery, and the Japanese company Sharp was the first to commercially produce an electric calculator.

なぜ、Q ロボット王国になったのですか？

日本では、世界で使用されている工業用ロボットの約7割が生産されています。また、工業用ロボットに限らず、1999年にはソニーが世界初の自律型エンターテインメントロボット＝アイボを販売したほか、1986年から本田技研が研究に着手していた二足歩行ロボットも実用化に近づいているなど、日本のロボット開発は常に最前線を進んでいます。日本では、ロボットを「産業の効率化」という目線だけでとらえず、「夢」とともに開発している部分も大きいと言えるでしょう。

1920年に「ロボット」という言葉をはじめて使ったのは、チェコスロバキアの作家カレル・チャペックですが、日本では、1951年に漫画界の金字塔的作品である『鉄腕アトム』が手塚治虫によって生み出され、1979年にはロボットアニメの名作『機動戦士ガンダム』が放送開始されました。

アトムが「人の心を持つロボットの象徴」であれば、ガンダムは「人が操作する実用ロボットの象徴」になっています。このアトムやガンダムに追いつくことが研究者たちの夢の原型になっているのかもしれません。

なぜ、Q 食料自給率がこんなに低いのですか？

日本の食料自給率は約40％で、先進国のなかでも最低レベルの水準となっています。国土が狭いうえに、非常に多くの人口を抱えているという基本的な問題点が、その背景にあるのはもちろんです。

また、産業構造の変化によって、農地面積が減少を続けていることも問題視されていますが、それ以上に大きいのは「日本人の食生活の変化」だと指摘されています。

かつての食卓においては、魚や野菜を使った和食がメインになっていましたが、現在では肉類がメインになっていて、若年層を中心に魚離れの傾向が見られます。

■ Why is Japan known as the robot kingdom?

Japan produces approximately 70 percent of the world's industrial robots. But not being satisfied with that, in 1999 Sony began selling the first autonomous entertainment robot, Aibo. The humanoid robot that Honda has been working on since 1986, which can walk on two legs, is approaching commercialization. Thus Japanese robotics continues to lead the field. In Japan, however, robots are seen not just as a means of improving industrial efficiency, but also as the pursuit of a dream.

The word "robot" was first used by the Czech writer Karel Čapek in 1920. In Japan, Osamu Tezuka produced his monumental manga *Astro Boy* (*Tetsuwan Atomu* in Japanese) in 1951. 1979 saw the first telecast of the anime masterpiece *Mobile Suit Gundam*.

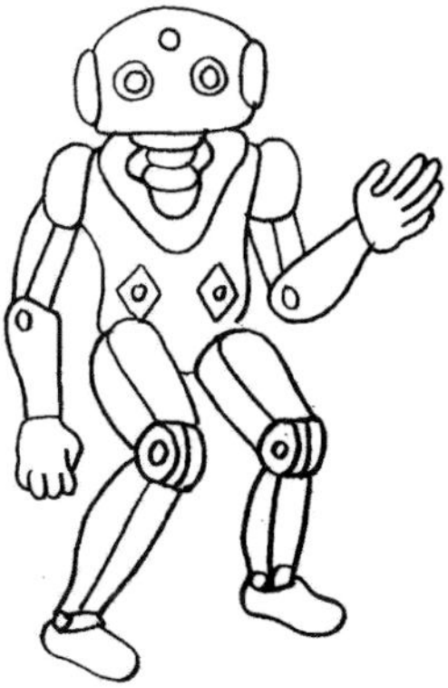

If Astro Boy is the most outstanding example of a robot with a heart, Gundam is the supreme example of a robot that can be used by human beings. It may be that for Japanese researchers engaged in robotics, these two robots represent the essence of the dream they are pursuing.

■ Why is Japan's food self-sufficiency so low?

Japan's food self-sufficiency rate stands at 40 percent, the lowest of any industrially advanced nation. The basic factor behind this problem is, of course, that Japan's population is too large for the country's land area.

A further problem is the continued decrease of agricultural land due to changes in the industrial structure of the country. An even more serious issue is the change in Japanese eating habits.

Traditionally the Japanese diet consisted principally of fish and vegetables, but recently it has come to center on meat, with the young leading the trend away from fish.

Surrounded by the sea, Japan has always been rich in fishery

国土を海に囲まれた日本は、魚資源には恵まれてきましたが、畜産の歴史は浅く、国土的にも不向きといえます。そのため、食肉の輸入が増えているのはもちろん、家畜の飼料用穀物の輸入までもが増えています。これによって、穀物自給率などはますます低い数字になっているわけです。

Qなぜ、100円ショップの品物はあんなに安いのですか

店内にあるすべての商品を一律100円で販売しているのが100円ショップです。CDやゲームソフトまで登場していて、「どうして、こんなものまで100円で売れるのか？」という商品も少なくなく、老眼鏡などは100円ショップのヒット商品のひとつになっています。

もちろん、100円ショップで売られている商品にしても、きちんと利益が出せるように工夫されています。その基本は、大量発注によって単価を低く設定しているということです。さらに、商品の製造を人件費の安い中国などで行なっている点も見逃せません。

また、工場の閑散期に製造を依頼して、製造料の値下げを交渉することなどもあるようです。さらに正社員をあまり採用しないで、パートを増やすことで人件費も下げているショップもあります。薄利多売方式は、このように成立しているわけです。

resources, but its history of raising livestock is short. Geographically the country is unsuited to raising livestock. It is not surprising that meat imports should continue to rise. This also applies to the importing of feed grain, which forces the grain self-sufficiency rate down even further.

■ Why can ¥100 shops sell things so cheaply?

It goes without saying that a ¥100 shop is a store in which every item is priced at ¥100. You may wonder how some items, such as CDs and game software, can be sold at such low prices. Recently bifocals have been one of the hottest-selling items.

Even at ¥100, each item is calculated to produce a profit. The key is to order in volume and keep the unit price down. Also, we shouldn't overlook the fact that manufacturing is done in countries like China where labor costs are low.

Further, it seems that another means of keeping costs low is to negotiate the price down by having the manufacturing done at a slow time of the year for the factory. Some shops don't hire many full-time employees but rely on part-timers, thus keeping labor costs down. This is how a high-volume low-margin business is set up to make a profit.

16 衣

なぜ、「着物」をもっと着ないのですか？

かつての日本では、着るものすべてを「着物」と呼んでいましたが、明治時代（1868-1912）以降、洋服を着る人が増えたため、洋服、和服と区別するようになり、着物といえば和服を指すようになりました。

戦後、和服を普段着にする人は減っていき、現在では、旅館の仲居さんなどのように仕事で着る必要がある人以外はほとんど着なくなりました。とくに若い人たちが和服を日常着ることはまったくなく、着るのは結婚式や成人式などの特別な日に限られています。

この理由としては、和服が非常に高価であることや動きにくいこと、簡単に洗えないことなどが挙げられます。また、和服を着るのがとても複雑で難しいのです。

ただし、和服のなかでも安価で、着るのが難しくない「浴衣」というものがあり、最近は夏にこれを着る若い人たちが増えています。

なぜ、和服では「左前」を嫌うのですか？

和服を着る際、右手側の衣を先に体につけて、それから左側の衣を重ねる方法を「右前」といいます。和服ではこの右前が正しく、その逆である「左前」にすることは絶対にいけません。外国映画で着物を「左前」に着た

Clothing

■ Why don't Japanese wear kimonos more often?

In old Japan, all clothing was known as a "kimono" (literally, "things to wear"). At the beginning of the Meiji period (1868-1912), however, the number of people wearing Western clothes increased, and so a distinction was made between Western clothes (*yōfuku*) and Japanese clothes (*wafuku*). At this time, "kimono" came to chiefly mean the full-length gown worn by both men and women.

After the end of World War II in 1945, the number of people who wore kimonos on a daily basis declined. At present, aside from chambermaids at Japanese inns and other people required to wear kimonos because of their work, almost no one wears them every day. In particular, young people never wear Japanese clothes, except at weddings and special occasions like the Coming-of-Age Day ceremony.

Some reasons for this are that kimonos are very expensive, that they restrict bodily movement, and that they are difficult to wash. Lastly, the kimono is complicated and a bother to put on.

There is one exception, however. That is the yukata, which is an informal kimono for summer wear. It is cheap and easy to put on. Recent summers have seen more and more yukata being worn by young people.

■ Why is the kimono folded right over left?

When putting on a kimono, the right side is folded over the body first, then the left side. In Japanese this is called *migimae* ("right front"), and it is considered the correct way to wear a kimono. The opposite way, with the left side going first, is called *hidarimae* ("left

日本人が出てくることがありますが、日本の作法ではこういうことは絶対にありえません。

どうして右前が正しい作法になったかについてはいくつかの説があります。まず719年に法令で、着物は右前で着るようにと義務づけられたこと。これは当時の先進国であった中国の風習に倣ったものだそうです。それから日本人には右利きが多いため、そのほうが着やすく動きやすかったためだとも考えられています。また、死者を弔うときにはこの逆で、左前の着付けをするため、生きているのに左前にすることは縁起が悪いと敬遠されているのです。

洋服の場合は、男性は右前、女性は左前ですね。これは19世紀後半に定着したようですが、理由は分かっていません。

Qなぜ、こんなに制服が多いのですか？

日本では多くの組織や企業、学校などで制服が規定されています。「組織への属性を明らかにすること」などが目的になっているものと考えられます。日本的な国家主義を感じさせるということで制服に対する反発もありますが、その利点もいくつか挙げられます。

たとえばデパートなどの店舗において、店員が制服を着ていれば、店員と客の区別がつけやすいので便利です。また、工場などで衣服が汚れやすい職業でも汚れが気になりません。

企業などでは、女性だけに制服が適用されるケースが多いのですが、ジェンダーフリーの立場からの批判が強くなってきたため、服装を自由化する企業も増えています。ただ、そうなると今度は、毎日の服装を考えなければならなくなるので、女性社員の中にも制服廃止を喜ばしく思ってない人は少なくないようです。学校でも同じことが言え、制服を廃止する傾向が見られますが、保護

front") and is just not done. In movies made abroad, when Japanese characters appear, they are sometimes wearing their kimonos in the "left front" fashion. This is absolutely unacceptable according to Japanese etiquette.

There are several theories as to why *migimae* is correct. First, a 719 government ordinance declared that kimonos should be in the *migimae* style. This ordinance was apparently issued so as to keep Japan in step with the practices of the most advanced country in the region at that time, China. Another possibility is that most Japanese are right-handed, and the kimono is easier to put on and easier to wear if in the *migimae* style. Furthermore, the kimono of the deceased on view at a funeral is done in the *hidarimae* fashion, and so it is considered bad luck for a living person.

Of course, with Western clothing, men follow the *migimae* style, women the *hidarimae*. This has been the custom since the latter half of the nineteenth century, although it is unclear why.

■ Why do so many people wear uniforms?

Uniforms are mandatory at many Japanese institutions, corporations, and schools. The purpose is to show clearly that the individual belongs to that particular organization; that is, it shows the person's affiliation. Some object to uniforms because they bring back memories of Japanese nationalism.

But uniforms do have some merits. For example, at department stores and other retail establishments, it is convenient to be able to distinguish at a glance between customers and clerks. In factories and other places where clothing is likely to get soiled, uniforms are less of a worry than ordinary clothing.

In some organizations, only women are required to wear uniforms, and this has come under considerable criticism from a gender-neutral point of view, with the result that more corporations are making clothing a matter of choice. However, if uniforms are done away with, then women employees have to worry about what they are going to wear each day, and for that reason some women are not

者からは「経済的負担が増える」という懸念の声も上がっています。

なぜ、Q 女子中高生は水兵のような服を着ているのですか？

これは「セーラー服」と呼ばれる制服です。女子生徒の進学率が高くなりはじめた明治時代には、袴を着用して通学するのが一般的でした。ところが1921年に、はじめて女子学生の制服としてセーラー服を採用した女学校が出ると、これが全国に広まっていったといわれています。

海軍の制服としてセーラー服を制定したのはイギリス海軍ですが、その後に日本の海軍でもこれを採用していました。また、イギリスでセーラー服が海軍幼年学校の制服に採用されたことから、19世紀末から20世紀のはじめにかけて、ファッションとしてのセーラー服が世界的にも広まっていったのです。

そうした中での採用だったわけですが、この頃には男子学生が陸軍の軍服に似た詰め襟の学生服を着用するようになっていたので、やはりそれに倣ったのではないかとも考えられています。

なぜ、Q 小学生はみんなランドセルを背負っているのですか？

日本ではかなりの割合の小学校で、通学鞄としてランドセルが指定されています。ランドセルのルーツは、兵士が背負う布製の「背のう」だったとされています。オランダ語でランセルは背負い鞄を意味しますが、それがなまってランドセルになったのです。

明治時代に、皇族や華族の子どもたちが通う学習院に

entirely happy with the abolishment of uniforms. There is the same trend to do away with uniforms in schools, but some parents are concerned that this will create an additional burden on their household budgets.

■ Why do students at junior high schools for girls wear uniforms resembling sailor suits?

These uniforms do, in fact, go by the name of "sailor suits." In the Meiji period (1868-1912), when girls began to go on to higher levels of education, they generally wore *hakama* (a kilt-like garment with wide pleats) to school. But in 1921 one girls' school decided on the sailor suit as its uniform, and this spread throughout the nation.

The British navy was the first to adopt the sailor suit as a uniform, with the Japanese navy following its lead sometime later. After being adopted at the British officer cadet school, the sailor suit spread throughout the world during the late nineteenth and into the twentieth century.

It was during this period that girls' schools began to adopt the sailor suit. It was also about this time that boys' schools adopted a uniform that resembled an army uniform with a standup collar, so it may have been that the girls' schools were playing catchup.

■ Why do all elementary school children carry knapsacks?

A knapsack is mandatory at many Japanese elementary schools for carrying books and supplies on the way to and from school. The origins of the knapsack are said to be the cloth backpack used by the Japanese army. In Japanese this knapsack is called a *randoseru*, which is apparently a mispronunciation of the Dutch word *ranseru*, which means "a pack for the back."

おいて、布製の背のうが通学鞄として利用されていました。そして、のちの大正天皇（1879-1926）となる皇太子が学習院に入学する際、当時の内閣総理大臣・伊藤博文（1841-1909）が箱型の背負い式鞄を特別に作らせて献上したのが、現在のランドセルの原型となったと言われています。学習院では、こうしたランドセルがその後も使われていましたが、高価なものだったため、全国に普及したのは戦後になってからのことでした。

多くの必要品が入るうえに、両手が自由に使えるランドセルは小学生に適した鞄だと言えるでしょう。ヨーロッパなどでも、背負い式鞄が小学生の通学に使われることが多く、韓国の小学生もランドセルに似た革製鞄を使う子が多いようです。

Q なぜ、こんなにブランド物が好きなのですか？

日本にショップを開く海外メーカーが後を絶ちません。海外の一流品メーカーにとっては日本が巨大マーケットになっていて、ルイ・ヴィトン製品などは、日本の成人女性の２人に１人が持っているというのですから驚かされます。

とくに女子大生には人気ですが、収入がないはずの学生が、海外では上流階級の婦人しか持たない一流品を身につけているのですから、外国の人がびっくりするのも無理ありません。

こうした商品を買う人たちは「品物が良くて長持ちする」と理由を口にしますが、それ以上に「みんなが持っているから」という心理が大きいのではないかと考えられます。周囲と同じものを持ち、同じふうにしていることで安心感を持つ人が多い国民性は否定できません。また、明治以降の西洋化の流れのなかで「海外製品信仰」のようなものが生まれましたが、それが現在でも消えていないものとも考えられます。

In the Meiji period (1868-1912), at the Peers School, which was established exclusively for the imperial family and the aristocracy, students at first used a cloth backpack. Later, when the crown prince, who would later become Emperor Taishō (1879-1926), entered Peers School, the then Prime Minister, Itō Hirobumi (1841-1909), had a special box-like leather backpack made and presented it to the prince. This became the prototype for the present-day *randoseru.* This type of knapsack continued to be used at Peers School, but since it was expensive, it wasn't widely adopted in other schools until after World War II.

Knapsacks are suited to elementary school children, considering how much the knapsacks can hold and the fact that the children's hands are kept free. It appears that many European children also make use of such backpacks, as well as a good number of South Korean children, whose leather backpacks resemble the *randoseru.*

■ Why do Japanese like brand name products so much?

There seems to be no end to the establishment of brand name stores in Japan by top foreign firms. Japan is a huge market for these top brand companies. It's astonishing to hear, for instance, that one out of every two Japanese women have a Louis Vuitton product.

These brand name goods are especially popular with female university students, who, you would think, have little ready cash. Visitors to Japan are understandably surprised, then, when they see these students wearing top-quality brand name products that only the very rich wear abroad.

The people who buy these products reasonably argue that they are of good quality and long-lasting, but one can't ignore the psychological factor of wanting what everyone else has. It can't be denied that the Japanese as a people tend to feel comfortable when they are doing what everyone else is doing. Furthermore, starting with the effort to Westernize in the Meiji period, a tendency to idolize Western goods developed, and that tendency has not altogether disappeared.

17 日本食

なぜ、すき焼きが代表的な日本料理なのですか？

日本では長い間、肉食が避けられていました。7世紀には天武天皇（631?-686）が最初に肉食を禁じ、8世紀には、仏教への信仰が厚かった聖武天皇（701-756）が牛馬の肉食を禁止しています。そうした背景があったため、魚以外の肉が日本人の食卓にのぼることはほとんどありませんでした。

本格的な肉食文化は、明治維新（1868年）の近代化によってようやく始まったといえます。この頃、のちにすき焼きという名前が定着することになる「牛鍋」が生まれ、もてはやされました。また、政府も1200年以上も続いた肉食禁止令を廃し、一転して肉食を奨励しました。これが近代化、西洋化の象徴として捉えられていたのです。

かつてアメリカでは『SUKIYAKI』という日本の曲が大ヒットしましたが、『上を向いて歩こう』が原題であるこの曲は、すき焼きとはまるで関係がありません。アメリカのレコード会社の社長が日本で食べたすき焼きの味に感動したのが曲名の由来だと言われています。

なぜ、天麩羅はポルトガル発祥なのですか？

今では日本料理の代表になっている天麩羅ですが、実をいうとその起源は定かではありません。日本に油料理を伝えたのは中国とされているので、そうした料理が原型になっているとも考えられます。ただし、戦国時代にポルトガルの宣教師によって伝えられた料理が起源と考

■ Why is sukiyaki so special?

Meat-eating has long been avoided in Japan. Under the influence of Buddhism, Emperor Tenmu was the first to ban the eating of meat in the seventh century, and in the eighth century Emperor Shōmu banned the eating of beef and horse meat. This tendency continued through history, with the result that the Japanese diet has long consisted almost entirely of vegetables and fish, with very little meat.

The custom of eating meat started in earnest in the Meiji period (1868-1912) with the beginning of the modernization of Japan. It was then that a "steamboat" dish (*gyūnabe*), later to be known as sukiyaki, made its appearance and attracted a good deal of attention. The government revoked the ban on meat-eating that had been in place for over 1,200 years and, entirely reversing course, began to promote the practice instead. This was seen as a symbol of the modernization and Westernization of the new Japan.

Some time ago, a Japanese song by the name of *Sukiyaki* was a hit in the United States, but in fact it had nothing to do with the dish. The original title is "Looking up as I walk." The American title came about because the president of the recording company had enjoyed eating sukiyaki while in Japan.

■ Why is tempura said to come from Portugal?

Tempura is now considered a typical Japanese food, but in fact its origins are unclear. Since cooking in oil came to Japan from China, it would seem reasonable to assume that the prototype of tempura was developed at that time. However, it is widely thought that tempura was originally brought to Japan by Portuguese missionaries

えるのが一般的です。天麩羅の語源もはっきりしませんが、ポルトガルで斎日を意味する「temporas」だとする説もあります。この説によれば、キリスト教には鳥獣肉を食べずに魚と卵を食べるようにする斎日があり、その際に宣教師が食べていた料理が元になっているのではないかと見られています。

いずれにしても、中世までの日本では油が貴重品だったため、天麩羅が大衆料理として広まったのは江戸時代以降のことでした。もともとは海外から伝えられた料理だったものを、日本人好みにアレンジしたのが天麩羅だと言えるでしょう。

Qなぜ、お寿司は世界中に広まったのですか？

寿司の起源は、ご飯の中に塩味をつけた魚を漬けておくことで発酵させた保存食です。これは紀元前4世紀頃から東南アジアで食べられていたもので、日本に伝わったあとには、地域ごとに作り方の工夫を凝らした「熟鮨」として広まっていきました。この熟鮨ではかなり長い間発酵させたのち、ご飯の部分をのぞいて魚の部分だけを食べます。独特な臭いがします。

そのうち魚といっしょにご飯も食べる方法が考え出されました。ご飯を発酵させるかわりに、酢を使って味をつける「早鮨」です。最初のうちは、おにぎりのような大きなものだったそうです。ひとくちサイズの「握り寿司」が登場したのは、江戸時代末期になってからのことでした。

その後、にぎり寿司は高級料理になっていきましたが、近年になって、寿司を握る機械や回転寿司などが開発され、一気に身近なものになりました。回転寿司とは回転するベルトの上に各種の寿司が置かれ、客は好みのものをとって食べて、値段は食べた皿の数で決まるものです。

最近では世界にも進出して人気を博し、外国の人たちが生魚を食べるきっかけとなっています。またそれぞれ

during the period of Warring States (1467-1568). The etymology of the word "tempura" is also unclear, but it is said by some to come from the Portuguese word *temporas*, which refers to a period when missionaries refrained from eating meat. According to this theory, the fish and eggs that the missionaries ate on these days became the foundation for what would later become tempura.

In any case, cooking oil was a precious commodity until the Edo period (1603-1867), and so it wasn't until then that tempura became popular among the common people. In conclusion, we can safely say that tempura is a foreign import that was adapted to suit Japanese tastes.

■ Why has sushi spread around the world?

Sushi originally consisted of fish cured with salt and fermented in rice. It was a form of preserved food. It had been eaten in Southeast Asia since around the fourth century BC. After being introduced into Japan, this type of sushi underwent regional changes and spread to all parts of the country as *narezushi*. With *narezushi*, the fish is fermented with rice for a relatively long period of time, and then eaten after the rice has been removed. It has a distinctive smell.

In the course of time, ways were devised so that the rice could be eaten with the fish. The next step was to add vinegar to the rice instead of fermenting it, and this was called "fast sushi." At first, the size of the sushi was apparently about that of a "rice ball" (*onigiri*), and it was only near the end of the Edo period (1600-1868) that the smaller bite-size portions of today's sushi (*nigirizushi*) came into being.

Sushi eventually became a rather expensive, high-class cuisine. All that has undergone a quick change in recent years with the appearance of sushi-making machines and conveyor-belt sushi restaurants, making sushi affordable for everyone. Conveyor-belt sushi (also called rotation or revolving sushi) refers to restaurants that have a revolving "line" on which plates of various kinds of sushi are placed. Customers take what they wish, and are charged by the

の国のテーストに合わせた寿司も考案され、カニ肉とアボカドとキュウリをまいた「カリフォルニア・ロール」などという傑作も生まれました。

食べ方はもちろん自由でいいわけですが、箸を使わず、手で持ってひっくりかえし、醤油を魚の方につけて食べるのが正しい作法とされています。

Qなぜ、ニセモノ食品が多いのですか？

日本が誇る（？）技術のひとつに、ニセモノ食品の製作があります。食べられないものとしては、レストランのショーウインドーに並んでいるメニュー・サンプルが挙げられます。本物ソックリにできたサンプルを見ながらどれにしようかなと楽しむものですが、メニューが読めない外国人にとっても助けになっているようです。ですから、このサンプルは日本みやげとしても人気商品のひとつになっています。

食べられる「ニセモノ食品」作りでも、日本の技術はいろいろなものを生み出しました。まずは魚肉ソーセージです。畜肉が高価だったころに、安い魚肉を使って作ったソーセージは大ヒット商品となり、日本の食生活を魚中心から肉食へ移行させる原動力にもなりました。

最近では、カニ肉をまねた「カニカマ」が世界的なヒットになりましたし、ニセモノのイクラも「本物に近い味」ということで人気がでています。そのうちにキャビアなんかも出てくるかもしれません。

Qなぜ、インスタント・ラーメンは世界的になったのですか？

インスタント・ラーメンは現在の日清食品の創業者、安藤百福氏が1958年に発明したもので、「チキンラー

number of empty plates they have.

It hasn't been too long now since sushi became popular overseas, giving people of various countries the opportunity to acquire a taste for raw fish. As time went on, sushi was created to suit local tastes, such as the wonderful California roll, consisting of rice, crab, avocado, and cucumber.

Sushi is often eaten with chopsticks, and of course there is nothing wrong with that. But using the fingers to pick up the sushi, turn it over, and dip the fish side into the soy sauce is actually considered to be traditionally correct.

■ Why is there so much fake food?

One technological innovation that Japanese can (perhaps) be proud of is fake food, that is, food replicas. These inedible models are lined up in restaurant windows to serve as examples of what is on the menu. Customers can have fun looking at these exact replicas and then decide what to order. For foreign visitors to Japan who can't read the menu, these models are a big help. In fact, fake food like this is apparently a favorite item among tourists to take home as souvenirs.

There is also fake (imitation) food that is edible, another range of products produced by Japanese technology. One example is fish meat sausage. When meat was expensive and fish cheap, fish meat sausage was invented and became a huge hit, in effect paving the way for the Japanese diet to move from being fish-centered to more meat-centered.

Recently, imitation crab meat (Kanikama) made a worldwide splash, and imitation salmon roe is praised as tasting almost like the real thing. What will come next? Perhaps imitation caviar.

■ Why have instant noodles become a worldwide phenomenon?

Instant noodles (instant ramen) were the invention of the founder of

メン」が最初でした。現在では全世界で作られていて、年間約850億食が消費されています。日本からの輸出は年間約8700万食と、消費量のなかでは大きな割合を占めてはいません。それでも、世界各地で生産されているインスタント・ラーメンのなかには、日本企業が現地生産しているものや、現地の企業と提携して作っているものが少なくありません。

どうしてこれだけの人気が得られたのかといえば、日本の味を押し付けたのではなく、各国の好みに合った味をそれぞれに提供していった結果だと言えるでしょう。箸を使い慣れていない欧米ではフォークで食べやすいように麺を短くしたり、回教国ではスープにブタの脂を使わないようにするなどの工夫もしています。

また2005年には国際宇宙ステーションでも提供され、宇宙進出もはたしました。2007年に安藤氏が亡くなったときには、ニューヨーク・タイムズ紙が「ミスター・ヌードルに感謝」と、その功績をたたえています。

Qなぜ、日本のご飯には味がついていないのですか？

たしかに味がついていない食べ物なんて、欧米の人たちにとっては初めての体験でとまどうようです。日本人の食事はご飯という主食とおかずという副食からなりたっていて、そのふたつが口の中で混じりあってはじめておいしい食べ物になるのです。こういう食べ方をするためには、ご飯に味がついていない方がいいわけです。

このため日本人の生活はつねにお米が中心になってきました。将軍が大名たちに与えた領地も「石」という単位で表されますが、これはひとりの人間が1年間生きていけるお米の量を示しています。また、侍たちの給料もお米で支払われていました。

昔の人は副食が乏しかったため、現在の人よりも大量

Nisshin Food Products, Momofuku Ando. Chicken-flavored ramen was the first to be marketed. Instant noodles are now produced throughout the world, and are being consumed at a rate of 85 billion servings per year. Japan exports about 87 million servings a year, which is not a significant percentage of the whole. Still, of all the instant noodles produced worldwide, a significant proportion is made by Japanese companies producing the product locally or through tie-ups with local firms.

As to why instant noodles became this popular, it wasn't by forcing people outside of Japan to adapt to Japanese flavoring, but rather by providing the flavoring that best suited the tastes of each country. Other adjustments were also made. In regions where chopsticks are not used such as Europe and the United States, the noodles are made shorter so that they can be more easily eaten with a fork. In Islamic countries, pork is not used in the soup.

Furthermore, in 2005 instant noodles made an appearance on the International Space Station, taking their first steps into outer space. When Momofuku Ando passed away in 2007, the *New York Times* praised him for his achievements in an article entitled "Appreciations; Mr. Noodle."

■ Why isn't Japanese rice flavored?

It is true that rice in Japan is an unflavored food. As such, it may be a first-time experience for Westerners, and therefore a bit confusing. A traditional Japanese meal is principally made up of rice, and secondarily of vegetables and fish. It is when the two of these come together in the your mouth and mix together that you can be said to be eating a flavorful meal. When food is eaten in this way, it is best if the rice is not flavored.

Rice has long been the centerpiece of Japanese life. In the Edo period, the land that the shōgun granted to the daimyō (feudal lords) was measured, not by area, but by how much rice it could produce. The unit of measure was called a *koku* and equaled the amount of rice that one person needed as food for one year. Payments to samu-

のごはんを食べました。詩人の宮沢賢治（1896-1933）は「一日ニ玄米四合」を食べると詠いましたが、これはお茶碗によそえば10杯分くらいになるでしょう。

なぜ、Q 毎日、味噌汁を飲むのですか？

味噌汁は中世・室町時代から作られるようになったと言われています。その後、日本では「一汁一菜」と呼ばれるように、ご飯のほかに、味噌汁などの汁物を一品、ほかのおかずを一品つけた食事をとるのが一般的になっていきました。

まず、主食のご飯には味がついていないので、汁物があったほうが食べやすいということがありますが、それ以上に大きいのは栄養的な問題です。味噌は、大豆から作られていますが、大豆には良質のたんぱく質が豊富に含まれています。日本では肉を食べることがほとんどなかったので、重要なたんぱく源だったわけです。また、味噌には塩分も含まれているので、汗を流す労働に出かける前後に飲むのに適していました。

なぜ、Q 納豆はあんな匂いがするのですか？

納豆は、外国人が苦手にすることが多い日本食の代表になっています。刺身は10人に7、8人は好きになるのに対し、納豆が好きになる人は1人か2人にとどまるようです。

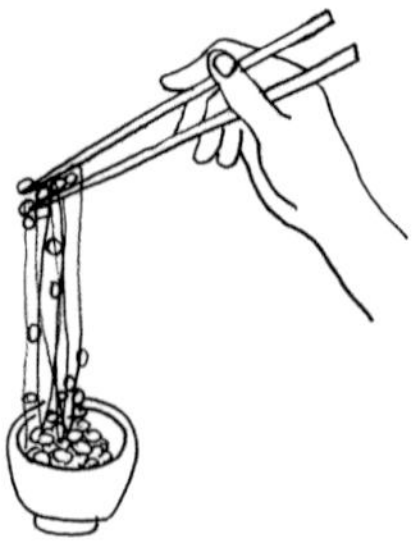

独特の匂いはありますが、腐っているわけではなく、納豆菌によって大豆を発酵させた食品です。ただ日本人でもあの匂いが嫌いという人がいて、最近は匂いをおさえた納豆も登場しました。

納豆がどのように生まれたかははっきりしていませんが、弥生時代（BC300頃－AD300頃）にはすでに食べられていた可

rai (their salaries) were also paid in rice.

In the past, fish and vegetables were not as plentiful as they are now, and as a result Japanese then ate much more rice than we do today. In one of his poems, Kenji Miyazawa (1896-1933) wrote that a person might eat ten bowls of rice a day, which is much more than anyone would consume today.

■ Why do Japanese drink miso soup every day?

Miso soup first made its appearance in the medieval period (1185-1568). Thereafter a Japanese meal came to be generally referred to as "one soup, one vegetable," meaning that other than the main component of rice, there should also be miso soup and one other item, either a vegetable or fish.

First, since rice is unflavored, it is much easier to eat with soup than without. But more important than that is the matter of nutrition. Miso is made from soybeans, and soybeans are a rich source of good protein. Since Japanese didn't eat much meat back then, soybeans were an important source of protein. Since miso also contains salt, drinking miso soup before and after doing heavy, sweaty work was beneficial to the health.

■ Why does *nattō* smell so bad?

Nattō is the leading Japanese food disliked by foreigners. Seven or eight foreigners out of ten like sashimi, but only one or two out of ten like *nattō*.

No mistake about it, *nattō* does have a distinctive smell, but that doesn't mean it's rotten. It comes from the fact that *nattō* is produced by fermenting soybeans with a rice straw bacterium called *Bacillus subtilis natto*. There are also Japanese who dislike its smell, and recently a variety of *nattō* has appeared that is less smelly.

How *nattō* came into being is not clear, but it seems very likely that it was eaten as long ago as the Yayoi period (300 BC-300 AD).

能性が高いと見られています。そうした長い歴史を持ちながら、関東以北や九州ではよく食べられていたのに対して、関西地方ではあまり食べられなかったという傾向がありました。最近では関西でも食べられるようになりましたが、まだ苦手な人も多いようです。

納豆は「体にいい食べ物」です。ビタミンB^{2}が豊富なうえに、最近では、納豆に含まれるナットキナーゼという酵素が血液中の血栓を溶かす作用を持つものとして注目されています。

Q なぜ、こんなにたくさん醤油を使うのですか？

醤油は日本料理の味つけの基本ですから、たしかにたくさん使います。外国の人が日本にやってきて日本料理に馴染んでいくのも、言いかえれば醤油に馴染んでいくということでしょう。豆腐に醤油をかけただけの冷奴をおいしいと思うにはある程度の時間が必要なのです。アメリカでは豆腐にドレッシングをかけたり、シロップをかけて食べたりするのが一般的です。

ところが最近では、和食ブームの影響で海外での醤油の需要が高まり、輸出が増えて、アメリカでは現地生産も行なわれています。一方日本国内では和食を作る機会が減りつつあるうえに、製品化された麺つゆや割下の影響で、醤油の消費が減っているというのは皮肉です。

Q なぜ、刺身がこんなに好きなのですか？

周囲を海に囲まれた日本では、全国各地で新鮮な魚が獲れます。そのため、世界中で食の起源となっていたはずの「生食」の習慣がそのまま残ったものと考えられます。醤油が普及する以前は、さまざまな味付けがなされていましたが、江戸時代から生の魚に醤油をつける刺身が人気を集めるようになっていきました。

フランス料理などはとくにそうですが、世界的に見れ

Even though *nattō* has a long history, it was traditionally eaten mostly in the Kantō region and northward, as well as in Kyūshū, but not much in the Kansai region. It has recently gained some popularity in Kansai, but there are still a lot of people who would prefer to do without it.

Nattō is a healthy food. Aside from being rich in vitamin B^2, it has recently attracted attention because of an enzyme called *nattokinase* that reduces clotting in blood vessels.

■ Why is so much soy sauce used in Japanese food?

Soy sauce is the basic seasoning in Japanese food, so it stands to reason that a lot is used. When foreign visitors say they have grown accustomed to Japanese food, it means, in effect, that they have gotten used to soy sauce. It takes a while before a newcomer to Japan begins to think that *hiyayakko* (a block of cold tofu) with soy sauce tastes good. In the United States tofu is generally eaten with some kind of syrup or dressing.

Recently, however, due to the fad for Japanese food, the consumption of soy sauce abroad has increased, exports have grown, and soy sauce is being locally produced in the United States. On the other hand, Japanese food is being less and less made in Japanese homes, and with the use of commercialized noodle soup, the consumption of soy sauce has, ironically, gone into a decline.

■ Why do Japanese like sashimi so much?

Since Japan is surrounded by the sea, fresh fish can be caught almost anywhere in the country. The custom of eating food raw, which was the original way that food was eaten all over the world, has almost entirely disappeared, but in Japan, apparently because of the easy availability of fresh fish, this custom survived. Before soy sauce became widely used, raw fish was prepared in various ways, but from the Edo period onward, sashimi with soy sauce became by

ば、できるだけ工夫を凝らした料理がもてはやされる風潮があります。しかし、日本食では「できるだけ手を加えず、食材が持っている本来の味を生かすこと」が大切にされています。新鮮な食材が手に入る場合は当然ですが、もともとおいしいものをわざわざ違う味にする必要はないという発想です。そうした意味でも、いたってシンプルな料理方法の刺身は、もっとも洗練された料理だと言うこともできるでしょう。

最近のフランス料理の新しい傾向（ヌーベル・キュイジーヌ）として刺身がとり入れられているのも、こういう発想法からきているのです。

Qなぜ、刺身はいつも大根の上に載っているのですか？

刺身に添えてある野菜や海草を「ツマ」といいます（関西地方では「ケン」と呼ぶこともあります）。これは、ステーキの皿に、添え物としてニンジンやポテト、クレソンなどがつけられていることと意味合いは似ていて、色のバランスを考えた盛り付けであると同時に、口直しの食べ物になっています。

大根のほかに海草なども利用されますが、白い大根を使うことでは、赤い刺身とのコントラストが美しく映えます。また、大根には消化を促進する成分が多く、殺菌作用もあるので、生食の添え物としては最適の食材と考えられているわけです。

Qなぜ、刺身にわさびをつけるのですか？

わさびの香りが魚の生臭さをおさえ、その辛さが刺身の味を引き立ててくれるからです。日本人でも、醤油にわさびを溶かして刺身につける人が多数派になっていますが、刺身にわさびを直接載せて食べたほうが、よりおいしく食べられます。

far the most popular way.

Almost anywhere you look in the world—but particularly in France—the tendency is to be as ingenious and elaborate as possible in the preparation of food. But with Japanese food the most important thing is to maintain the taste of the original ingredients, without adding anything. Of course, this particularly applies when the food is fresh, but the basic philosophy is that there is no need to change the taste of something that tastes good in its natural state. In that sense, you can say that sashimi, which is supremely simple, is the most refined of dishes.

This philosophy can be seen in the latest French cuisine, *nouvelle cuisine*, which has incorporated sashimi into its new style of simplicity and elegance.

■ Why is sashimi always served on a bed of daikon?

The vegetables and seaweed served with sashimi are called *tsuma* (or sometimes *ken* in the Kansai region). The function of *tsuma* is somewhat similar to the carrots, potatoes, and watercress that are served with steak; that is, they provide a nice balance in terms of color while also serving to refresh the taste buds.

In addition to daikon (East Asian giant white radish), seaweed and other vegetables are also used, but the pink sashimi appears to particularly good effect when seen against white radish. Daikon also aids in digestion and inhibits microbe growth, and in that sense is the perfect complement to raw fish.

■ Why is sashimi eaten with wasabi?

The reason that sashimi is eaten with wasabi (Japanese horseradish) is that the aroma of the wasabi counters the fishy smell of the sashimi, and the hotness of the wasabi brings out the flavor of the fish. Many Japanese mix the wasabi with soy sauce to form a kind of dip, but putting the wasabi directly on the sashimi actually produces

また、わさびには殺菌効果があるので、生食である刺身につける香辛料としては、非常に適しているわけです。刺身を食べる習慣が日本から伝わった台湾では、日本人でもビックリするほど山盛りのわさびをつけて食べます。国が違えば味覚も違うようです。

なぜ、Q 「生け作り」が食べられるのですか？

生きた魚を刺身にして、それをもとの骨の上にならべて、魚のかたちに整えて出す料理を「生け作り」といいます。日本人は、刺身は新鮮なほどおいしいと考えているので、こうした盛り付けによって、少し前までは生きていた魚を調理したばかりだということを強調するわけです。実際、口や尾がピクピクしているのが新鮮そのものということで喜ばれます。

しかし、魚といえばほとんど切り身しか食べない外国の人は、生きていた姿が想像される「生け作り」に拒絶反応を起こします。これは、常日頃の食習慣の違いから起きてくるギャップと考えるしかないでしょう。

the best eating experience.

Wasabi also has the effect of inhibiting microbe growth, and so it is nearly perfect as a spice for raw fish. In Taiwan, where the habit of eating sashimi was picked up from Japan, so much wasabi is used that even Japanese are astounded. It just goes to show: different countries, different taste buds.

■ Why do you eat fish that is still alive?

The preparation of living fish for eating is called *ikezukuri* (or *ikizukuri*). This consists of a live fish being selected, sliced into thin pieces of sashimi, and then the pieces of sashimi being placed back on the bones of the fish to recreate its original shape. Since, for Japanese, the fresher the sashimi the better, this re-creation of the fish is done to emphasize the fact that the fish was alive until just moments ago and has only now been prepared for eating. Sometimes the mouth or tail is still moving, which is welcomed as a sign of how fresh the fish is.

For foreigners who have only eaten fish that has been prepared in advance, the thought of eating a living fish may be disgusting. This can only be thought of as the result of differences in daily eating habits, a matter of what one is used to, or not used to.

18 食事のマナー

なぜ、Q 日本料理ではスプーンを使わないのですか？

日本では箸だけで食事をするのが基本となっています。もともと箸は、中国、韓国、日本、ベトナムといった漢字文化圏で使われていました。ところが他の3国ではスプーンも併用しているのに、日本だけはスプーンを使っていないのです。

これは、汁物などを食べる際に、手で器を持って、口まで運ぶ食べ方が習慣化されていたので、スプーンを使う必要がないからですが、それにしても日本だけないのは不思議です。

日本で箸が使われるようになったのは7世紀のはじめです。中国に遣隋使を送った際に、食事に箸が使われているのを知りました。そこで、日本人も同じ作法ができるようにしようと考えた聖徳太子が、箸の使い方を訓練させたのが始まりと言われています。

正しい箸の持ち方は意外にむずかしく、おとなでも持てない人がいるくらいで、子供に教えるのに苦労しています。しかし、正しく持てば食べ物が摑みやすく、美しくも見えるので、後世に伝えていきたいものです。

なぜ、Q 箸と茶碗は、個人の所有物が決まっているのですか？

ふつうの皿や碗などは家族共通で使っているのに、箸と茶碗だけは家族のものでも気持ちが悪くて使えない……これが一般の日本人の心理でしょう。外で食事するときには、そこで出された茶碗でもなんとも感じないの

Table Manners

■ Why don't Japanese use spoons?

Chopsticks are the basic utensil for eating in Japan. From olden times, chopsticks have been used in China, Korea, Japan, and Vietnam, the so-called Chinese culture sphere. As it happens, however, spoons are used along with chopsticks in the other three countries, but not in Japan.

The reason for this is that when Japanese eat soup, they pick up the bowl and bring it up to their mouths, making employment of a spoon unnecessary. That stands to reason, but it is still somewhat puzzling as to why only Japan should be left spoonless.

Chopsticks came to Japan at the beginning of the seventh century when Japanese ambassadors to the Sui Dynasty came back with news of the custom. Prince Shōtoku thought chopsticks would be a good custom to adopt, and he encouraged people to practice how to use them.

The correct way to hold chopsticks is not as easy as it seems. There are even some adults who don't do it the way it should be done, and they find teaching their children how to do it somewhat of a chore. However, if done correctly, it makes picking up food much easier, and it also lends an element of elegance to the meal. It is a custom well-worth passing on to later generations.

■ Why do Japanese have their own personal chopsticks and rice bowls?

Even though most plates and bowls may be used by anyone in the family, when it comes to chopsticks and rice bowls, each person has their own personal items. Using another family member's chopsticks

ですから、思えばおかしな心理です。
昔の日本では箱膳といって、１人分の箸や茶碗などを収容する箱型のお膳が使われていました。自然に食器が個人所有になっていたわけで、それが現在の習慣として残ったのではないかと考えられています。また、いろいろなものの中に「神」が宿っていると考えていた日本人が、自分の命をつないでくれる主食、「ご飯」を食べる食器に特別な感情を持ったからだという説もあります。
箸や茶碗にはいろいろな長さ、大きさ、色柄があるので、自分に合ったものを使うようにしているということも理由のひとつかもしれません。

Qなぜ、漆器が「ジャパン」と呼ばれるのですか？

欧米では漆器を「ジャパン」と呼んでいます。これは主な素材として木や紙を使う漆器が日本的なものと思われたため、磁器の「チャイナ」に対して、こう呼ぶようになったものです。
漆器は東アジア一帯で作られていて発祥の地は分かっていません。中国では紀元前16世紀〜紀元前10世紀くらいの遺跡から漆器の一部が発見されていますが、日本でも縄文時代（BC10000年-BC4世紀）には作られていたことが分かっているので、「ジャパン」と呼んでもらっていいのかもしれません。

Qなぜ、お酒をあんなに小さな器で飲むのですか？

日本でも、ビールや氷を入れた焼酎などはグラスやジョッキで飲みます。小さな器で飲むのは日本酒だけです

or rice bowl just wouldn't feel right, or this is the way most Japanese think, in any case. When eating outside the home, however, no one feels the least bit odd about using the rice bowl or chopsticks provided for their use. In that sense, it doesn't seem to make sense.

At mealtime in the past, Japanese placed in front of each individual a low box-like table (*hakozen*) that contained the chopsticks, rice bowl, and other utensils used by that individual. The idea that the utensils in the box belonged to that individual developed from this custom. This seems to have come down to us today in the form of personal chopsticks and rice bowls. Another theory is that since Japanese then thought that spirits inhabited many and various things in the world, they also thought that the utensils that allowed them to eat rice and survive in the world were somehow special.

Another reason may be that since chopsticks and rice bowls come in various sizes, shapes, and patterns, it is only natural that people should want to use what they feel suits them personally.

■ Why is lacquerware called "japan"?

In the West, lacquerware is called "japan." This naming arose because lacquerware made with wood or paper was thought to be typically Japanese, just as porcelain was thought to be Chinese and therefore called "china."

Lacquerware has long been made throughout the entire East Asian region, and it is unclear exactly where it originated. In China, lacquer fragments have been discovered in a site dating from the sixteenth century BC to the tenth century BC. In Japan, it is known that lacquerware was made in the Jōmon period from 10,000 BC to the fourth century BC. From that perspective, maybe it's alright if lacquerware is call "japan."

■ Why do you drink sake in such small cups?

Although other alcoholic beverages such as beer are drunk in glasses or mugs, sake is the only drink drunk out of a small cup. You might

から、欧米でウイスキーなどをストレートで飲む際に用いるショットグラスと同じようなものだと考えていいでしょう。日本酒を飲むのに使われている器を「猪口」と言います。これはもともと、料理のなかのちょっとした一品を盛るのに使われていた器でしたが、江戸時代（1600-1868）からお酒を飲む際にも使われるようになりました。

日本酒のアルコール度数が高くなるとともに小さくなっていったとも言われています。また昔は、同じ盃をやりとりしてお酒を飲む「献酬」という作法があったため、小さい方がよかったのかもしれません。猪口にはさまざまな種類があるので、コレクターズ・アイテムとしても人気があります。

Qなぜ、すぐにお酌をするのですか？

もともとは客人や目下の者に対するふるまいの意味が強かったのですが、仲間意識を高めるための自然な行為になっていき、それがいつのまにか、酒席におけるマナーになっていったのです。こうした席で自分でお酒をついで飲むのは「手酌」といって不作法なこととされています。ですからいつでも相手のコップがカラにならないように注意していなければなりません。最近ではこんなかたくるしいことを嫌い、自分でついで飲む人も多くなりました。

欧米では女性が男性にするお酌は敬遠されるのに対し、日本にはそうした考え方がありません。そのため、お酌がビジネスマナーと教育される一方で、セクシャル・ハラスメントだとも指摘されるようになっています。

Qなぜ、こんなに自動販売機があるのですか？

海外から来た人にとっては、街角に立ち並ぶ自動販売機が異様に見えるようです。日本の自動販売機総数は500万台を超えており、性能面や販売商品の多様さにお

think of it as the equivalent of a shot glass for drinking whiskey straight. This cup is called a *choko*, and its original use was to contain some small bit of food. It came to be used as a sake cup in the Edo period (1600-1868).

It is said that as sake's alcohol content got higher, the smaller the *choko* became. There was also a custom in which one cup was passed around to all participants. Maybe a small cup was more suited to this custom than a large one. There are many kinds of *choko*, and collecting them is quite popular.

■ Why do you pour one another's drinks?

Pouring another's drink was first done for guests or for those who were lower on the social ladder. Then it was done as a natural way of bonding between equals. From there, it became part of the etiquette of drinking in general. In fact, pouring one's own drink is seen as bad manners. This requires that attention be constantly paid to other people's glasses or cups, to see that they don't become empty. Recently, however, some people think this custom is too rigid, and prefer to pour their own drinks.

In the West, it is not considered proper for women to pour men's drinks, but this custom does not apply to Japan. However, while pouring other people's drinks is taught as part of business etiquette, there are those who view it as a type of sexual harassment.

■ Why are there so many vending machines?

In the eyes of many visitors to Japan, the great number of vending machines lining the streets seems to present a particularly strange sight. The number of vending machines in Japan now totals over

いて独自の発展を見せています。ここまで多くなった最大の理由は、１日中外に出しておいても商品やお金を盗られることのない治安の良さにあるでしょう。

商品としては、タバコやコーヒー、ジュースなどのほかに、ポタージュやお汁粉などもあるし、さらにはコンドームやストッキングまでもが売られています。最近では缶入りおでんが登場し話題になっています。

5,000,000, and both in terms of functionality and the variety of goods sold, the vending machine is evolving in unique ways. The biggest reason for its growth is the fact that even if they are left outside all day long, they are not broken into and goods and money are not stolen—in other words, because of the excellent public safety.

Among the goods sold are cigarettes, coffee, juice, and other similar items, which can be taken for granted; but also things like potage and *oshiruko* (a dessert consisting of azuki bean soup with a rice cake known as *mochi*), as well as condoms and stockings. Recently canned *oden* (a stew particularly popular in winter) has attracted a good deal of attention.

19 住

なぜ、家に入るとき靴を脱ぐのですか？

古くから日本では、テーブルや椅子、ベッドはあまり用いず、畳に直接座ったり、畳の上に布団を敷いて寝る生活様式をとってきました。外を歩いてきた靴のまま家に上がれば、土や泥が畳につくことになります。直接座ったり布団を敷いたりする場所が汚れることに抵抗を覚えるのは自然な感覚といえるでしょう。とくに汚れを落としにくい畳に土足で上がることは絶対のタブーになっています。

もちろん、欧米でも床に座ったり寝ころんだりすることはあるわけですから、靴をぬぐというのは「うち」と「そと」を峻別する日本人の特殊な心理が関係していると考えられます。「うち」は清潔で「そと」は不潔だから、「そと」の汚れを「うち」に入れないようにしようというわけです。

また欧米人は足が大きいので靴をぬぐのにいちいちヒモを解かなければならない、だから靴を脱がないのだという説もあるのですが、真実はわかりません。

なぜ、「遊びにきてね」と言いながら、招待してくれないのですか？

外国の人から見れば、かなり失礼なことにも思えるのでしょうが、日本人の感覚からすれば、こうした言葉は、挨拶に近いもので、本気で言っているわけではないのです。

極端にいえば、人と別れるときに英語で「Have a nice day」と言うのに近いのかもしれません。相手に対

Housing

■ Why do Japanese take off their shoes in the house?

Traditionally, the Japanese house did not make much use of tables, chairs, or beds. People sat directly on the tatami and slept in a futon laid out there. If they came in from outside without removing their shoes, the tatami would, of course, get dirty. It is only natural that people should dislike the place where they sit and sleep to get dirty. In particular, dirt is difficult to remove from a tatami, so walking on the tatami in one's shoes became taboo.

However, Westerners also sit or lie on the floor—without removing their shoes—so we are left to consider if Japanese remove their shoes because of the special distinction they make between "inside" the house and "outside" the house. Inside the house is clean, the outside is dirty, and so an effort is made to keep the dirtiness from the outside from coming inside.

One theory that has been presented for why Westerners don't remove their shoes is that they have big feet and it is too much trouble to undo their shoelaces every time they come inside. I wonder if this is actually true.

■ Why do Japanese say, "Come over sometime," when they don't really mean it?

From a foreigner's perspective, this must seem impolite or even insulting, but from a Japanese perspective, saying "Come over sometime" is just a standard way of saying goodbye; it is not meant to be taken literally.

In a sense, it might be seen as similar to saying, "Have a nice day." "Come over sometime" is simply meant as a sign of good feel-

する好意を示す言葉として用いられることが多いため、日本人同士で使った場合、それを聞いた方は実際に誘われたとは受け取りません。具体的な日にちを言われて初めて本気の招待だとわかるくらいです。

また、最近でこそ、ホーム・パーティーなどを開く人も増えてきましたが、日本の住宅事情は悪く、広いリビングや庭がある家に住んでいる人はあまりいません。マンションなどに住んでいる場合は、ちょっと大きな声を出しただけで、隣人からの苦情が出ることも少なくないので、気軽に人を招けない事情もあるわけです。

ただ、海外の人はこういう言葉を最大級の親愛の情とうけとめ、期待しているのですから、一度言ってしまったら招待するのがマナーでしょう。

Qなぜ、日本のトイレにはシャワーが付いているのですか？

もともとシャワー付きトイレは、医療施設や福祉施設で用いるためにアメリカから輸入していたそうです。しかし、日本人は清潔志向が強いので、一般向けに発売しても需要があると考えたことから製品開発が進められ、1980年から発売が開始されました。

当初は贅沢品とも見られていましたが、やがて普及していき、現在では累計で2000万台以上が販売されています。

ホテルや旅館でもシャワー付きトイレが増え、公共施設や一般会社でもつけるところがでてきました。そうしたなかで多機能化も進み、便座を暖かくできる製品のほか、消臭機能や消音用の音楽機能などが付いている製品も登場しています。

来日したアメリカの歌手、マドンナが「日本の暖かい便座が懐かしかった」と話したエピソードは有名です。それにもかかわらず、アメリカなどではこうした製品が普及しないのは、「暖かい便座は他人が使ったばかりのようで気持ちが悪い」などという心理的な問題や、火傷

ing toward the other party, and is employed quite often with that meaning, so Japanese usually don't take it seriously among themselves. Only if a specific date is brought up do Japanese believe that they have received an invitation.

Recently the number of Japanese giving parties in their homes has increased, but it is still true that housing in Japan is not all that good, and not that many Japanese have spacious living rooms or yards. And in condominiums and apartment buildings, you are likely to get complaints from the neighbors if you make a little more noise than usual. The fact is that you can't easily ask people over without considering the consequences.

However, since foreigners take these words so seriously and interpret them as a sign of friendship, once you have invited them, it is only proper that you follow up on it and have them over.

■ Why do Japanese toilets have built-in water jets?

At first, toilets with built-in water jets—that is, toilets with an integrated bidet—were imported to Japan from the United States for use in hospitals and welfare institutions. Since Japanese have a fetish for cleanliness, some people thought there should be a market for such toilets, and development commenced. A commercial product was produced and went on sale in 1980.

At the beginning they were considered luxury items, but gradually they became accepted. At present, more than 20,000,000 have been sold, many under the trademark Washlet.

Such toilets have increasingly been installed at hotels and inns, and some public facilities as well as private firms have also adopted them. In the meantime, the toilets themselves have become multifunctional, including some that warm the toilet seat, some that remove odors, and some that play music to drown out indelicate sounds.

When the singer Madonna returned for a visit to Japan, she famously remarked on how much she had missed the warm Japanese toilet seats. Nevertheless, these toilets still haven't caught on in such

などによる訴訟問題が起きることを懸念しているためではないかと考えられます。

なぜ、Q トイレ専用のスリッパがあるのですか？

下水道が発達する以前の日本のトイレは、便壺に大小便を溜めておき、いっぱいになったらそれを汲み出すという形式が一般的でした。そのため、トイレは家屋から離れたところに作られることが多く、トイレに行くためには履物を使う習慣があったのです。

また、少し年配の人なら、今でもトイレのことを「ご不浄」と呼ぶ場合があります。この言葉は「きれいではない、神聖ではない」ということを意味しています。衛生的な意味だけではなく、感覚的な意味も持っていて、古い時代にはトイレは魔物の出入り口と考える発想もあったくらいです。

昔からそうした考え方があったため、トイレは「うち」のなかでも特殊で不潔な空間と捉える感覚があり、現在でもそれが残っているわけです。最近ではお風呂とトイレが一体化しているユニットバスも増えてきましたが、それに対して嫌悪感を持つ人も少数ですがまだいます。

こんなことから「不浄」な場所専用のスリッパが必要なのです。トイレ用スリッパを履いたまま部屋に戻ってこないように注意してください。

countries as the United States, apparently because a warm toilet seat reminds them of the person who sat there before them and other such psychological issues. There is also the worry that one might be sued if the toilet should overheat someone's rear end.

■ Why does the restroom have its own pair of slippers?

Before the development of a proper sewage system in Japan, human waste was deposited in tank-like containers that were emptied when they became full. Such facilities were built away from the house, and to reach them, footwear was necessary.

Some elderly Japanese may still refer to the toilet as "the unclean," meaning that it was both unsanitary and "impure." This is to be taken not only in a hygienic sense, but also in a psychological sense. In days gone by, it was even thought that the toilet was the gateway through which demons made their way in and out of this world.

Even if the toilet was within the confines of the house, it was still regarded as a special place that housed "impurities." That feeling still exists somewhat today. Even with the combined bath and toilet units that are increasingly being installed today, there are still some people (though a minority) who strongly object to this practice.

So, this is the reason that slippers are used to enter this special "impure" area. Of course, these slippers are not to be worn in any other part of the house.

20 宗教

なぜ、Q お寺と神社の両方にお参りするのですか？

日本のもともとの宗教である神道は多神教です。山や川といった自然、あるいは風や火といった自然現象を神格化したアニミズム的な神が信仰対象になっていました。そして、古代の国づくりに貢献したと見られる人物なども神格化していき、それぞれを祀っていたのです。

そんな中で、中国から朝鮮半島を経由して仏教が入ってきたときにも、それまで信仰していた神々は排斥しないで、仏教と共生できるようにしていきました。「神道」という名前も「仏教」と区別するために生まれてきた言葉でした。神道と仏教を折衷させたことを「神仏習合」と呼びます。仏教を排斥しようとした一時期を除けば、日本ではこうしたかたちの信仰が長く続けられてきました。

仏教は世界宗教であり、神道は日本人のための民族宗教だとも言えます。仏教発祥の地、インドにおいても、ヒンドゥー教の神々を否定するのではなく、信仰の対象として仏教に取り入れた歴史が見られますが、それに近いかたちがとられたわけです。こんな事情から、お寺と神社の双方にお参りすることにも違和感はないわけです。

■ Why do Japanese worship at both Buddhist temples and Shintō shrines?

The native religion of Japan, Shintō, is polytheistic; that is, it has many gods, not just one. In Shintō, natural objects such as rivers or mountains were treated as gods. Phenomena such as wind and fire could be seen as gods as well. This view of nature is called animism. Even human beings—people who made great contributions to the country or were outstanding in some other way—could be considered gods.

When Buddhism came into Japan from China through Korea, the Japanese people did not give up the gods they had worshiped up to that point, but instead tried to live with both religions. In fact, the word "Shintō" (literally, "Way of the Gods") came into being to distinguish that religion from Buddhism. The attempt to combine Buddhism and Shintō into one system is called Shintō-Buddhist syncretism. Aside from one period when there was an attempt to eliminate Buddhism, Japan has long lived with these two religions, side by side.

While Buddhism is a major religion with followers throughout the world, Shintō is a folk religion, confined almost solely to Japan. When Buddhism was first developing in India, it did not deny the gods of Hinduism, but rather incorporated them into Buddhism. Something similar to this is what happened in Japan. Today, Japanese feel completely comfortable worshiping at both Buddhist temples and Shintō shrines.

なぜ、Q 結婚式は神道でやるのに、お葬式は仏教であげるのですか？

現在ではこのようにするのがトレンドになっていますが、もともと日本において、結婚式は宗教的儀式ではありませんでした。かつては、それぞれの家などで、時代ごとの作法に基づいた祝いの宴などが開かれていただけだったのです。

神社で結婚式が挙げられるようになったのは明治時代（1868-1912）になってからのことで、大正天皇が1900年に神前結婚式を行ったことから、この形式が全国に普及していきました。

現在では、キリスト教式の結婚式が増えていますが、もともと結婚式に対する宗教意識が薄いために、ウェディングドレスへの憧れなどから、こうした選択がなされていると言えるでしょう。

葬式に関しても、仏教との結びつきはそれほど歴史が古いものではありません。葬式が仏式で行われ、寺院の境内にお墓が建てられることが定着したのは江戸時代以降のことでした。これは、キリスト教の布教を取り締まるため、すべての人たちを近くのお寺に檀家として帰属させる制度がつくられたことがきっかけになっています。

もともと、仏教は葬儀を行う習慣を持つ宗教ではなかったのです。ただし、死を「穢れ」と考える神道に対し、仏教にはそうした考えがありません。こんな背景もあって、中世頃から人の死に対して僧侶が一定の役割を果たすようになってきたことから、仏教と葬式が結びついたと考えられます

神道やキリスト教の様式で葬式が行われることもありますが、それは故人やその家族がそれぞれの宗教に帰依している場合が多く、数は多くありません。また仏前結婚式も、多くはありませんが行われています。

■ Why are weddings held at Shintō shrines and funerals held at Buddhist temples?

For some time now, this has been the general trend. But in the distant past, Japanese wedding ceremonies had no religious meaning. Each household simply had a gathering to celebrate the event according to the standards of the time.

It was in the Meiji period (1868-1912) that weddings first came to be held at Shintō shrines. After Emperor Taishō (1879-1926) was married in a Shintō ceremony in 1900, the practice spread throughout the country.

At present, Christian weddings are on the increase. However, since Japanese have never placed much importance on the role of religion in a wedding ceremony, the selection of a Christian church for the event probably has more to do with the attraction of such things as the wedding dress than anything else.

As for the relationship between funerals and Buddhism, the historical connection is not that old. It was only after the beginning of the Edo period (1600-1868) that funerals became established as a Buddhist ceremony and graves were situated within the temple grounds. What brought this about was the prohibition of Christianity. Part of this prohibition was that all Japanese had to become parishioners of a local Buddhist temple.

In fact, Buddhism was not a religion that had any particular traditions concerning funerals. However, it is true that while Shintō viewed, and avoided, death as an "impurity," Buddhism had no such concept. In any case, it was between the twelfth and sixteenth centuries that monks began to play a role in death rites and Buddhism became associated with funerals.

Christian and Shintō funerals are also held, but that is usually because the deceased person was, or his family are, believers. The number is not large. Likewise, Buddhist weddings, while not unheard of, are not numerous.

なぜ、Q 神社の前には鳥居があるのですか？

神社は「神の住まい」として建てられているので、鳥居は、人間の領域と神の領域の境界を分けている門だと言えます。その形や名前の起源については諸説あります。釈迦牟尼の遺骨（仏舎利）を祀った仏塔（ストゥーパ）を囲む門（トラーナ）からヒントを得たとも、日本の神話にルーツが求められるとも言われています。

なぜ、Q 神社で拝むときに手を叩くのですか？

この作法は拍手（かしわで）といい、古代においては、貴人に対しても手を打って拝礼していたため、それが神に対する作法として残ったと考えられています。拝む対象や神社によって、何度手を叩くかという決まりが変わってくる場合もあります。ただし、基本は「二拝二拍手一拝」で、まず２回おじぎをし、次に２回手をたたき、最後に１回おじぎをするというものです。

なぜ、Q 祭りのときに神輿を担ぐのですか？

日本の祭りの起源は、神様に来ていただき、いっしょになって飲んだり食べたりして楽しんだということです。そのときの歌や踊りが「神楽」です。

神輿の起源については諸説ありますが、「神々が移動するための乗り物」と考えられています。そのため、神社を模した形になっているものが多く、外国人に対しては「Portable Shrine（移動式神社）」と説明する場合もあります。激しく神輿を揺らしながら練り歩いたり、複数の神輿をぶつけ合ったりするなど、祭りによって作法が異なりますが、こうした行為は神に活力を与える意味を持っていると言われています。

■ Why is there a gate in front of Shintō shrines?

The shrine is the dwelling place of a god or gods, and the gate marks the dividing line between the world of the gods and the world of men. As for the shape and name (*torii*; literally, "bird place") of the gate, there is no definitive theory concerning their origins. Some say the shape is influenced by the gates in front of Asian Continental stupas (which are said to house the remains of Sakyamuni Buddha). Others say that the gate's roots are to be found in Japanese mythology.

■ Why do Japanese clap their hands when worshipping at a shrine?

In ancient times, apparently the hands were clapped as a sign of respect to people of high rank. This custom survived, it seems, in the form of clapping to show respect to the gods. Depending on the god in question and the particular shrine, the number of times that you are supposed to clap can differ. In general, however, the rule is bow twice, clap twice, and then bow once more at the end.

■ Why are portable shrines paraded around during festivals?

The original purpose of Japanese festivals was to invite the god or gods to come to the festival and eat, drink, and have a good time. The music and dance that accompany festivals is called *kagura*.

There are a number of theories concerning the origin of the portable shrine (*mikoshi*) carried around during festivals, but the most common one is that it is a vehicle for the god to move about in. Perhaps for that reason, most *mikoshi* take the shape of a miniature shrine. In some festivals the *mikoshi* are violently shaken as they are paraded about, and in other festivals several of them bang into one another. Each festival has its own way of doing things. But in general, this kind of spirited behavior is said to energize the god.

なぜ、Q 狐や実在の人物を祀る神社があるのですか？

キリスト教やイスラム教における神と、日本の神道における神では、その性格が大きく異なります。一神教と多神教では、神に対する考え方が異なるからです。

一神教における神とは、創造神、絶対神ですが、多神教の神がそうした性格を有していることはほとんどありません。また、一神教では神を唯一の絶対神と考えていることから他宗教に対して排他的な立場をとりやすいのですが、多神教は他宗教の神を受け入れやすい土壌を持っています。

仏教にも、その始祖・釈迦牟尼をはじめとした信仰の対象となる仏様たちがいますが、仏様、すなわち仏陀という言葉は「悟りを開いた者」という意味を持っています。言いかえれば、仏教とは信者の一人一人が「仏陀」になることを目指しているのです。つまり、仏様は神ではありません。

日本の神というものは、自然や自然現象、祖先、あるいは国づくりに貢献した人物などを神格化した存在です。江戸時代の国学者・本居宣長（1730-1801）は、神（カミ）とは「尋常ではないもの」「すぐれたもの」「畏れ多いもの」だと定義しています。ですから、いろいろなものが神になりうるのです。そんなことから考えても、英語のGODを日本語で神と訳したり、日本の神を英語でGODと訳すこと自体に無理があると言えるのでしょう。

狐が祀られているのは「稲荷神」ですが、稲荷神は穀物の神で、社の数は全国で３万を超えると言われます。そして、祀られている狐は「稲荷神の使い」であり、稲荷神そのものではありません。

また、神道では「祀られた人はすべて神」と考えます。歴史上有名な人物が祀られることが多いのですが、平安時代の貴族、菅原道真（845-903）や、明治時代の明治天皇（1852-1912）や軍人、東郷平八郎（1847-1934）などがその代表です。

■ Why are foxes and historical persons worshiped at Shintō shrines?

There is a big difference between the Christian or Islamic concept of "God" and the Shintō concept. This comes from the difference in thinking between monotheistic religions (religions that believe there is only one god) and polytheistic religions (religions that believe there are many gods).

In monotheistic religions, God is the creator of the universe and possesses absolute power. In polytheistic religions, the gods almost never have these characteristics. Since monotheistic religions believe that their god is the only god, and has absolute power, they tend to reject other religions and their gods. Polytheistic religions, on the other hand, are capable of accepting gods from other religions.

In Buddhism, beginning with the founder of the religion, Sakyamuni Buddha, there are many buddhas that serve as objects of worship. However, the word "buddha" refers to a person who has become enlightened (who has seen the light). And in Buddhism, each believer is striving to become a buddha. We can see from this that a "buddha" is not a "god."

In Shintō, aspects of nature, natural phenomena, ancestors, and people who have contributed to the country as a whole can be raised to the status of gods; that is, they can become gods. The Edo-period scholar Motoori Norinaga (1730-1801) defined *kami* (Shintō gods) as something beyond the ordinary, something marvelous, and something breathtaking. This makes it possible for any number of things to become gods. From this point of view, it doesn't make much sense to translate the English word "god" as *kami* in Japanese, or to translate the Japanese word *kami* as "god" in English. It just leads to misunderstanding.

Foxes are worshiped at Inari shrines. Inari is the god of rice and other grains. There are more than 30,000 Inari shrines throughout the country. The fox is the messenger of the god Inari, not the god itself.

In Shintō, historical figures can also have shrines built in their honor and therefore assume the status of gods. Many famous people

なぜ、Q イエス・キリストの墓が日本にあるのですか？

青森県三戸郡新郷村には「キリストの墓」とされる墓が立っています。これは、1930年頃に竹内巨麿という人物が発見したという古文書『竹内文書』の中に「十字架で磔にされたのはキリストの弟イスキリで、キリストは日本に逃れて106歳まで生きていた」という記述があったことから、それを探索して発見したとされるものです。

この新郷村は、かつて戸来（へらい）村と呼ばれていて、ヘブライが訛ったものではないかと考えられるなど、ユダヤ人の文化が伝えられていたと見られる点がないわけではありません。ただし、『竹内文書』の信憑性はどうかといえば、キリストだけではなくモーゼも来日していたとまで書かれているものなので、荒唐無稽と考えるのが一般的です。

なお、この新郷村には、古代の祭祀遺跡とされるピラミッドもあります。不思議な土地と言えるのは確かでしょう。

throughout history have been raised to the status of gods, such as the Heian-period aristocratic scholar Sugawara no Michizane (845-903), Emperor Meiji (1852-1912), and Fleet Admiral Heihachirō Tōgō (1847-1934), who shocked the world by defeating the Russian Baltic Fleet in 1905.

■ Why is Christ's last resting place said to be in Japan?

The final resting place of Jesus Christ is said to be in the village of Shingō, Aomori prefecture. The story goes that a person named Kyomaro Takeuchi discovered some old documents around 1930, now known as the Takeuchi Documents. According to these documents, it was not Jesus who was put on the cross but his younger brother, Isukiri, while Jesus escaped to Japan and lived to the age of 106. Based on this document, Takeuchi set out to find Jesus's grave, and he did.

Shingō village was previously known as "Herai," and this word is thought to be a mispronunciation of the word "Hebrew." This and other things leave one feeling that there may be some remnants of Hebrew culture in the village. However, as the Takeuchi Documents go on to say that Moses also came to Japan, their reliability has been called into question. The general view is that the Documents are complete nonsense.

Furthermore, there is a "pyramid" in the village that is supposed to be an ancient religious site. Whichever way you look at it, Shingō is a strange place.

21 風習

なぜ、Q たくさんの年賀状を送るのですか？

欧米のクリスマス・カードに似ているところもあるのでしょうが、年賀状に宗教性はありません。また、親しい人だけに限らず、仕事の関係者や親戚など、多くの人に出すのが習慣化しています。住んでいる場所が離れている知人などとは、年に１回やり取りする年賀状が唯一の交流となっているケースも珍しくないのです。

平安時代（794-1185）から、正月には新年の挨拶に行く習わしがあり、主君や上役、父母や親戚、知人や近隣の人のもとを訪ねて回っていました。それが1899年に年賀郵便制度が生まれて、これが普及してからは、実際に挨拶に行くのはごく一部の人だけにして、ほかの人たちには年賀状を送るようになったのです。

ただ最近は、e-mailを年賀状代わりにするケースも増えていて、年賀はがきの発行枚数は減少傾向にあります。それでも、2007年用年賀はがきは約38億枚発行されているのですから、約１億3000万人という人口を考えれば、かなりの数字だとは言えるのでしょう。

なぜ、Q お中元、お歳暮というプレゼントをするのですか？

中元はもともと中国の道教の行事で、半年間無事に暮らせたことを祝って祖先の霊を供養する日でした。それが日本に入ってきて、祖先や両親に食べ物を贈るような習慣が生まれたのですが、さらにお世話になった人にまで贈るようになったものです。

そして1911年に、百貨店の「三越」が「中元の進物はうちにご用命を」という広告をうってサマーセールを

■ Why do Japanese send out so many New Year's cards?

While Japanese New Year's cards probably have something in common with Western Christmas cards, New Year's cards have no religious meaning. Also, New Year's cards are sent not only to close friends but also to colleagues, relatives, and many other people. For friends and acquaintances who live some distance away, this may be the only time you communicate with them throughout the year.

New Year's greetings perhaps started in the Heian period (794-1185), when it was customary to visit one's lord, superior, parents, relatives, friends, and neighbors to express New Year's greetings. In 1899, however, with the birth of the postal system to print and deliver New Year's cards, the sending of cards became customary, and actual visits became less frequent. Most people ended up receiving a card rather than a visit.

Recently, the exchanging of email New Year's cards has increased, and the number of cards printed has gone down. Still, in 2007 3.8 billion cards were printed, which is quite a lot considering the population of Japan is only 135 million.

■ Why do Japanese send gifts in summer (*chūgen*) and winter (*seibo*)?

The custom of *chūgen* originally came from China and was a Taoist event. It celebrated having lived safely through half a year and served as a memorial service for ancestral spirits. In Japan the event called for sending gifts of food to one's parents and making offerings to ancestral spirits, and it later expanded to include sending gifts to people to whom one was somehow indebted.

ヒットさせたことから、ほかの百貨店もこれに追従していき、中元に贈り物をする習慣が定着したのです。中元は本来、「お盆」と重なる年中行事でしたが、現代人はほとんどそれを知らず、夏のプレゼント行事と考えています。

歳暮は、文字どおり年の暮れという意味の言葉です。１年間世話になった人に挨拶に回る「歳暮回り」という習慣があり、この際にちょっとした贈り物をするようになっていました。それが現代では、歳暮回りはごく一部にとどめて、宅急便などで贈り物だけを届けるようになったのです。

お中元にしてもお歳暮にしても、親しい人へのプレゼントというよりも仕事などでお世話になっている人に贈ることが恒例化しています。それがなかば義務のようにもなってしまったため、最近では、こうした習慣はなくそうとする動きも出てきています。

Qなぜ、お彼岸に墓参りをするのですか？

「彼岸」とは、春分・秋分の日の前後３日ずつの７日間のことです。彼岸とはもともと仏教用語で、煩悩を捨てて達する悟りの境地を意味しています。

春分・秋分の日には、太陽が真東から昇り、真西に沈むため、西方の彼方にあると考えられている極楽浄土に思いを馳せながら太陽に礼拝し、極楽往生を願う中国の習慣が起源になっています。

それが日本に伝わったあと、自分の極楽往生を願うのではなく、先祖の供養をする習慣へと変わったのだと言われています。

In 1911 the department store Mitsukoshi ran a very successful summer sale advertisement calling for people to buy their *chūgen* gifts at Mitsukoshi. Other department stores followed up, and the custom of sending *chūgen* gifts became firmly established. Originally, *chūgen* overlapped with Obon, the Buddhist summer festival to honor one's ancestors, but most people are no longer aware of this, believing *chūgen* to be simply a summer gift-giving custom.

Seibo (almost literally, "end of the year") originally referred to the year-end custom of visiting people one had become indebted to during the course of that year, and expressing one's gratitude to them. At that time, a small gift was presented. Now, the actual number of visits is cut short. Gifts predominate, being sent by overnight delivery.

Whether *chūgen* or *seibo*, the gifts are not sent to people one is actually close to, but rather to business associates or others one is indebted to in some way. This has become a convention and is more a duty than anything else. Recently, some have argued for doing away with such customs.

■ Why do Japanese visit the family grave during the vernal and autumnal equinoxes?

The day, or days, during the vernal and autumnal equinoxes when family graves are visited is called *higan*. *Higan* refers not only to the day on which the vernal and autumnal equinoxes fall, but also to the three days preceding and following that day. Originally a Buddhist term, *higan* (literally "the farther shore") refers to the state of enlightenment reached after all earthly distractions have been discarded.

During the two equinoxes, the sun rises due east and sets due west. Paradise is thought to lie due west, and so people prayed to the sun and hoped to be reborn in Paradise. This custom came to Japan from China.

In Japan, however, the custom changed from praying for one's own rebirth in Paradise to praying for that of one's ancestors.

なぜ、Q　「お盆」は7月と8月に2回あるのですか？

お盆は祖先の霊を祀る行事で、もともと7月13~16日に行われていました。日本では長いあいだ太陰太陽暦（旧暦）が用いられていましたが、明治6年にグレゴリオ暦（新暦）が採用されました。それによって、お盆は新暦では8月13~16日ということになったのです。

そこで、旧暦の日付けにそのまま従うかたちで7月13~16日をお盆とするか、新暦の8月13~16日をお盆とするかで、考え方が分かれていったのです。ただし現在では、7月13~16日をお盆としているのは古くから東京に住んでいる人たちくらいで、全国のほとんどでは8月13~16日がお盆と考えられています。

この頃には墓参りのために故郷に戻る人が多いため、普段はなかなか会えない親戚や旧友などとも再会しやすくなります。そこで、宗教行事というよりは国民的な慣習として、8月中旬に「お盆休み」をとることが定着していきました。これが日本人の「夏休み」です。

なぜ、Q　海や川にロウソク（灯籠）を流すのですか？

これは「灯篭流し」と呼ばれるお盆の行事のひとつで、お盆のあいだ家に帰ってきていた祖先の霊を送り返すために、死者の魂が乗っていると考えられる灯籠を海の向こうに流しているのです。灯籠は魂が行く道を照らしていることになります。

ただこれに関してはちょっとおかしなことがあります。というのは、仏教では先祖の人たちは「あの世」で仏様になっているので、そうそう気軽に帰ってはこられないはずだからです。このあたりには、死後の世界は地底や海の向こうにあり、祖先の霊は人間の招きに応じてこの世にやって来て人間と交歓するという神道の考えが入っているようです。

ですから「お盆」や灯籠流しは、仏教と神道が混交した中から発生した行事と言えるでしょう。

■ Why is Obon held twice, in July and August?

Obon is a Buddhist holiday to honor the spirits of one's ancestors. Traditionally, it was held from July 13th to the 16th. These days were set according to the lunisolar calendar, which Japan had long used. In 1873, however, Japan switched to the Gregorian calendar, according to which Obon would fall on August the 13th to the 16th.

So the question arose whether to follow the old calendar or the new one when celebrating Obon. Opinion was split for a while. These days, however, about the only people adhering to the old dates are Tokyo old-timers. Almost everyone else in the country has adopted the new calendar.

Since many people living in cities return to their parents' home in the country to visit the family grave, Obon is a good time to reunite with relatives and old friends that one usually doesn't have a chance to see. Rather than a religious festival, Obon has become an annual event, a part of ordinary Japanese life, taking place in the middle of August. It is the Japanese equivalent of a summer vacation.

■ Why are candles set afloat on rivers and in the ocean during Obon?

Tōrō nagashi (roughly, "lantern floating") refers to a custom that is part of Obon. During Obon, ancestral spirits return home to be with the family. When it comes time for them to leave, a lantern with candles is set afloat so that it floats out to sea. The ancestral spirits are said to be on this lantern, the candles lighting their way.

However, there is something a little odd about this tradition when seen from a Buddhist perspective. That is, according to Buddhism, our ancestors have already become buddhas and are living in Paradise. They don't come back to earth all that easily. However, in Shintō (the native Japanese religion) the dead live in the center of the earth or beyond the sea. Further, in Shintō the spirits of the dead return to earth and mingle with human beings if invited to do so.

So it seems that the customs of Obon and *tōrō nagashi* arose from the intermingling of Buddhism and Shintō.

なぜ、Q 大晦日には、除夜の鐘を108回撞くのですか？

12月31日を「大晦日」（1年の最後の日）といいますが、「除日」（旧年を取り消す日）ともいい、その夜が「除夜」（旧年を取り消す夜）というわけです。この除夜に、深夜0時を挟むようにしてお寺で撞かれるのが除夜の鐘です。どうして108回鳴らすかについては諸説ありますが、一般的には108というのは人間の煩悩の数だと考えられています。

煩悩とは人間の心身をわずらわせるもととなる「迷いの心」のことです。それを振り払った清らかな気持ちで新しい年を迎えようという意味を持っているわけです。古くから日本人は、眠らないで新年を迎えるようにしていて、除夜の鐘を聞きながら、お寺や神社にお参りする習慣があります。こうした正月のお参りのことは「初詣で」と呼ばれています。

なぜ、Q 結婚式を挙げていい日といけない日があるのですか？

日本では、毎日の運勢を「先勝、友引、先負、仏滅、大安、赤口」の6種類に分ける「六曜」が定着しています。365日すべてにこれがこの順番で振り分けられています。そして、このなかでもっとも運勢のいい「大安」に結婚式を挙げることが多くなり、もっとも運勢の悪い「仏滅」を避けるのが一般的になっています。

六曜は室町時代（1333-1568）に中国から伝わってきたものですが、その起源は定かではありません。古来の中国では、単に「天気の呼び方」として用いられていたにすぎないとも言われています。

いずれにしても、毎日の運勢を分けることには何の根拠もない俗信であるのは間違いありません。「仏滅」には、仏様が亡くなるという漢字があてられていますが、これももともとは同じ読み方で違う意味を持つ漢字（物

■ Why are temple bells struck 108 times at midnight on New Year's Eve?

December 31 is called *ōmisoka* (roughly, "big last day of the year") or *jojitsu* (roughly, "the day that gets rid of last year"), and the night of the last day of the year is called *joya* (roughly, "the night that gets rid of last year"). The temple bells that ring out just before and after midnight are called *joya no kane*. These bells ring out 108 times, and the question is why that exact number? There are a number of theories explaining why this is done, but the most widely accepted is that 108 is the number of "distractions" that human beings fall prey to.

"Distractions" are the mental states that cloud and confuse the human mind. Temple bells are struck 108 times in order to remove these "distractions" and make the mind and heart pure and "un-distracted" for the New Year. From olden times, Japanese have stayed up all night to greet the New Year, have listened to the temple bells, and have paid their first visits of the year to Buddhist temples and Shintō shrines. This "first visit" is called *hatsumōde*.

■ Why are there good and bad days to have a wedding?

There is a firmly established system in Japan called *rokuyō* ("six days") that tells which days are lucky and which are not. These days are called Senshō, Tomobiki, Senbu, Butsumetsu, Taian, and Shakkō, and they are assigned in this order to all 365 days of the year. Taian ("Great Peace") is particularly lucky and is often chosen for wedding days, while Butsumetsu ("The Passing of Buddha") is avoided as being the most unlucky.

This system was imported from China in the Muromachi period (1333-1568), but its Chinese roots are not clearly known. In ancient China, the system may have been a way of assigning names to different kinds of weather.

In any case, dividing the days according to whether they are lucky or not is just a superstition and has no foundation in fact. Take the day Butsumetsu. This word is now written with Chinese charac-

滅）があてられていたので、仏教ともまったく関係がないことです。

それでも、こうした慣習に逆らうのは、やはり気持ちがいいものではないのでしょう。現在でも、仏滅には結婚式を挙げないという慣習は残っているので、結婚式場では、仏滅の日の料金を大幅に下げる設定がなされているほどです。

また、友達をあの世に引っぱって行くという連想から、葬式を友引の日にすることも避けられています。

Qなぜ、4と9という数字は嫌われているのですか？

日本語で4は[shi]と発音されるので、同じ音となる「死」を連想させるものとして嫌がられています。同様に9は[ku]と発音されるので「苦」を連想させるとして嫌がられます。単に語呂合わせと言えばそれまでですが、日本には古くから、言葉には霊的な力が宿るとする「信仰」があるため、それに結びついてこうした考えが定着したものと考えられます。

西洋で不吉な数字とされている「13」と扱いは似ていて、ホテルなどの部屋番号や旅客機のシート番号から除かれるケースも見られます。とくに、死を避けたい気持ちが強い病院では、病室の番号から外されることが多くなっています。

Qなぜ、料理屋の前に塩を置いてあるのですか？

この塩は「盛り塩」と呼ばれ、店にお客さんや福を招く縁起物です。その由来は中国の故事にあると言われています。中国の始皇帝（BC259-BC210）は牛車で多くの妾のもとに通っていましたが、そのうちのひとりが始皇帝を自分のところで足止めしようとして、門前に牛の好きな塩を盛ったのが始まりだというのです。

ters meaning "The Passing of Buddha," but originally the word was written with different characters, with a different meaning, which just happened to have the same pronunciation. So actually there is no connection with Buddhism at all.

Still, people feel uneasy going against such superstitions, and even today the custom of avoiding weddings on Butsumetsu survives. As a result, wedding halls charge much less for ceremonies on Betsumetsu than any other day.

The same applies to Tomobiki ("Pulling a Friend"). Funerals are usually not held on this day because of the feeling that a friend may be "pulled" along with the dead to that other world.

■ Why don't Japanese like the numbers 4 and 9?

In Japanese, the number 4 and the word for "death" have the same pronunciation, *shi*, so the number 4 is considered unlucky by association. The number 9 has the same pronunciation as the word for "hardship," *ku*, and is seen as unlucky for that reason. You could say that this is just a coincidence, or that it is a kind of pun. But from ancient times, Japanese have believed that words have a spiritual power, as these examples show.

As with the number 13 in the West, you often find the number 4 removed from hotel rooms and passenger seats in airplanes. In Japanese hospitals in particular, 4 is avoided as a room number.

■ Why is there a little pile of salt in front of Japanese-style restaurants?

These little piles of salt are a kind of magic charm, and their role is to attract customers as well as good luck. They are said to have originated in ancient China. The first Chinese emperor, Shih Huang ti (BC 259-BC 210), had many mistresses. The story goes that in order to get him to stop at her place, one mistress put a pile of salt in front

また日本では、塩は「穢れ」を払う効果があると信じられています。お葬式に参列すると必ず少量の塩をわたされますが、これは帰宅して家に入る前に体にかけて死の「穢れ」を払うものです。店の前に盛り塩をするのも、店に「穢れ」が入ってこないようにするという意味もあるのでしょう。

力士が相撲をとる前に土俵に塩をまくのも同じ考えからですが、これには土俵の土を滑りにくくするということと、体をすりむいた際に治りが早いという効果もあるようです。

なぜ、バレンタインデーに女性が男性にチョコレートをあげるのですか？

バレンタインデーは世界各地に広まっていて、ローマ時代に殉教死した聖バレンタインの祭日といわれていますが、その起源は定かではありません。現在の欧米では、恋人たちがメッセージカードやプレゼントを贈り合ったり、愛を告白する日になっていますが、日本では「女性から男性へチョコレートを贈る日」というように形式を限定した習慣が根付いています。

世界的に見て、贈り手が女性に限られ、贈り物がチョコレートと決められているのは日本だけのようです。これは、1936年にモロゾフという製菓会社がバレンタイン・チョコレートの広告を出し、1958年に東京の伊勢丹というデパートでキャンペーンが行われたのが始まりとされています。その当時はそれほど反響がなかったといいますが、1970年頃からこの習慣が定着していきました。

of her gate. The emperor was riding an ox cart, and the oxen, liking salt, would stop to lick it. In that way the mistress could keep the emperor from going elsewhere.

In Japan it is also believed that salt has the power to remove "impurities." For example, if you attend a funeral, you will receive a small amount of salt as you leave. When you get home, you sprinkle the salt on yourself to remove the impurity that comes with being close to death. Putting salt in front of a restaurant may have a similar meaning, to keep impurities from entering the restaurant.

In Sumo, the wrestlers throw salt on the ring before wrestling, and this has somewhat the same meaning. Aside from the purifying factor, the salt makes the ring less slippery for the wrestlers, and if the wrestler should happen to scrape an arm or leg, he is likely to heal more quickly.

■ Why do women give men chocolate on Valentine's Day?

Valentine's Day is known almost everywhere in the world, and is said to be in commemoration of the martyred Saint Valentine in Roman times. However, the origins of Valentine's Day are not absolutely clear. In Europe and the United States, it is a day for lovers to send cards or presents to one another or to confess their love. In Japan, it has become strictly a day for women to give chocolate to men.

Only in Japan, it seems, is the giver limited to women, and the gift to chocolate. The roots of this tradition lie in the Valentine chocolate advertisement put out by the confectionary maker Morozoff Limited in 1936, and in the 1958 sales campaign carried out by the Tokyo branch of the Isetan department store. At the time, there was apparently little reaction to these efforts, but by 1970 the custom had become firmly established.

22 歴史

なぜ、Q

「日本」という国名になったのですか？

日本の国がいつごろから「日本」と呼ばれるようになったかは、はっきりとは分かっていません。ただし、有力な説のひとつとして、以下のようなものがあります。日本は古来、中国の歴史書などでは「倭」と呼ばれていましたが、この「倭」という言葉には「小さい」という意味があり、中国側の蔑みの意味が含まれていたのです。

そのため、この言葉を用いるのを嫌った日本人は、新たな国名を独自に摸索しはじめました。そんな中で注目されたのが、古代の政治家、聖徳太子が中国に宛てた国書に書いていた「日出処」（ひいずるところ）という言葉です。ここから転じて、「ひのもと」「日本」という言葉ができあがったというわけです。

なぜ、Q

海外ではジャパンなのですか？

これについては諸説ありますが、いちばんわかりやすいのは「ジッポン」説です。「日本」の「日」という字には「ニチ」「ジッ」という２つの読み方があります。それを中国では「ジッポン」と読み、それが転じて「ジャパン」になったというものです。

13世紀末に『東方見聞録』を著したマルコ・ポーロも、日本のことを「黄金の国ジパング」として紹介しましたが、この「ジパング」という呼び名も「ジッポン」と呼ばれたことに起因しているという説が有力です。

■ Why is Japan called "Nihon" by the Japanese themselves?

Nihon, or Nippon, is the official name of Japan in Japanese, but it is not exactly clear when this name first came into use. One of the most persuasive arguments is the following. In the earliest references to Japan in Chinese historical documents, Japan was referred to as "Wa." This word contained the meaning "small," and showed that China thought less than highly of Japan.

Japanese didn't appreciate this, so they began to search for another name for the country. In one official document of the seventh century, written by Prince Shōtoku and addressed to the emperor of China, Japan was referred to as the "the place where the sun rises." This was shortened to "sun origin," which is the literal meaning of "Nihon."

■ Why is Japan called "Japan" abroad?

There are a number of theories about how the word "Japan" came into use, but the easiest to understand is the following. The official name of Japan is Nihon, or Nippon, and is written in two Chinese characters: 日本. The first character can be read with an initial "n" sound or an initial "j" sound. Apparently the Chinese used the "j" sound, producing "Jippon" or "Jippan."

In the late thirteenth-century *Travels of Marco Polo*, Japan, the island of "endless gold," is referred to as Cipangu, which is probably based on the Chinese pronunciation "Jippon." At the very least, this seems to be the strongest argument.

なぜ、Q 卑弥呼のいた場所がわからないのですか？

3世紀半ば、日本においてはじめて統一国家的な体裁を保ったのが、卑弥呼と呼ばれる女王が統治していた「邪馬台国」と呼ばれる国です。この古代国家はさまざまな謎に包まれていますが、その第一は「場所が特定できない」ということです。

この邪馬台国については中国の『魏志倭人伝』という歴史書の中にしか記述が見られないのですが、それが不正確なのです。なにしろ記述どおりに考えれば、邪馬台国は海の上にあったということになってしまいます。

このため「邪馬台国がどこにあったのか？」という問題は、日本史上最大の歴史ミステリーとされ、学者だけでなく市井の研究家も巻き込み、さまざまな推測がなされています。現在では、本州中央部の奈良県にあったとする説と九州の福岡県ではないかとする説の2つが有力です。

なぜ、Q 京都や奈良にはお寺が多いのですか？

仏教を厚く信仰していた聖武天皇（701-756）は、仏教によって社会の不安を鎮めようと考え、8世紀半ばに奈良・東大寺に大仏を造立することを決めました。このように政治と仏教が強く結びつき、仏教文化が花開いた時代に日本の都は奈良にあり、その後まもなく京都に都が移されたため、京都や奈良には世界遺産や国宝に指定されている寺院や仏像が多く残されているのです。

また日本の大都市の多くは第2次世界大戦のとき、アメリカ軍の空襲で破壊されましたが、京都、奈良は無事でした。これは、日本の美術家、岡倉天心(1863-1913)のもとで学んだアメリカの美術史家、ラングドン・ウォーナー（1881-1955）のおかげと言われています。彼はこうした文化遺産を戦火から守ろうと考え、空爆すべきではない地域をまとめた「ウォーナー・リスト」を作って米政府に進言していたためと言われています。

■ Why is the location of the country Yamatai in dispute?

Yamatai is the name of the first political entity that could be called a nation in Japanese history. It existed in the middle of the third century and was under the control of a female ruler named Himiko (or Pimiko). There are many unsolved mysteries concerning this ancient country, the first of which is its location.

The only historical reference to Yamatai is in the Chinese *Records of Three Kingdoms* (297 AD), but the location given there is inaccurate. Following the *Records* directions, Yamatai would have existed in the middle of the ocean.

The true location of Yamatai has therefore become one of the biggest mysteries in the study of Japa-nese history. It has attracted the attention not only of scholars but also of amateur historians, producing various speculations. At present, the two locations that seem most likely are Nara prefecture in middle of Honshū and Fukuoka prefecture in Kyūshū.

■ Why are there so many temples in Kyōto and Nara?

Emperor Shōmu (701-756), who was a strong believer in Buddhism, decided to build a great statue of Buddha at Tōdaiji temple in Nara in order to bring peace to the nation. This connection between political power and religion led to a flowering of Buddhist culture in Nara, which was then the capital of the country, and later in Kyōto, when the capital was moved there. For this reason, there are many temples and Buddhist statues in Kyōto and Nara that have been designated World Heritage Sites or Japanese National Treasures.

Furthermore, most large Japanese cities were destroyed during World War II by American bombing, but Kyōto and Nara were not. The reason they were not bombed is said to be due to the art historian Langdon Warner (1881-1955), a student of the scholar Tenshin Okakura (1863-1913). Warner believed that cultural treasures should be protected from the ravages of war, and he drew up a list of regions that should not be bombed and presented it to the American government.

なぜ、Q 五重塔は1000年以上も立っていられるのですか？

奈良の法隆寺の五重塔、あるいは法起寺や薬師寺の三重塔は7世紀から8世紀にかけての創建と言われていますから、もう1300年も立っていることになります。木造できゃしゃな塔が、地震や台風にたびたび襲われる日本で1300年も立っているのは奇跡としか思えません。

ただこの奇跡にはタネも仕掛けもあるのです。まず細長くて5階、3階と高いのですから弱々しく見えますが、内部は普通の部屋にはなっていません。中央部は礎石から頂上まで巨大な心柱がつらぬき、その回りには建物を支える木組みがギッシリと詰まっているのです。このため頂上まで登れない塔もあるし、登れたとしても、木と木の間のわずかな空間につけられた垂直に近いハシゴを登っていくしかありません。

また心柱と回りの木組みは固定されていず、地震のときには別々に動くため倒壊しないと言われています。現代の超高層建築に使われている「柔構造」と同じ理論ですが、塔のメカニズムはまだ完全には解明されていません。

なぜ、Q 「世界初の長編小説」が日本で生まれたのですか？

西暦1007年頃に紫式部によって書かれた『源氏物語』は、世界最古の長編小説と言われており、現在でも日本人の多くはそのように考えています。しかし、こうした評価が正しいかについては疑問の声もあり、ローマ時代の作家、アプレイウスが書いた『黄金の驢馬』などに続く「古代長編小説のひとつ」と考えるべきだという指摘も出ています。それでも、『源氏物語』を「日本文学史上最高の傑作」とする評価は少しも揺るがず、今なお現代語訳や外国語訳が刊行されたり、映画化されるな

■ Why have wooden pagodas managed to survive for over 1,000 years?

The five-story pagoda at Hōryūji temple, the three-story pagoda at Hokkiji temple, and the three-story pagoda at Yakushiji temple, all in Nara, were all built during the seventh and eighth centuries. They have been in existence for over 1,300 years. That such slender pagodas, made entirely of wood, should survive 1,300 years of frequent earthquakes and typhoons is nothing less than a miracle.

But this miracle did not occur without reason. These three- and five-story pagodas may look weak from the outside, but the inside presents a different picture. First, there is a tall column that rests on a stone base and rises to the top of the pagoda. Around it are many jointed wooden parts that are loosely attached to the column and support the exterior structure of the building. Because of this mass of joinery, you cannot climb to the top of many pagodas, or if you can, it is only by climbing an almost vertical ladder squeezed in between all the wooden parts.

Since the joinery is not firmly attached to the central column, each part moves independently when there is an earthquake, ensuring that the whole structure will not come down in one piece. The "flexible structure" used in modern high-rise buildings is based on the same theory. However, it appears that these pagodas have still not revealed all their secrets.

■ Why was the oldest full-length novel in the world written in Japan?

The world's oldest novel, written around the year 1000, is said to be *The Tale of Genji* by Murasaki Shikibu. Most Japanese still believe this to be true, but doubts have been raised in certain quarters. For example, some critics think that the *Genji* should be ranked after the Roman writer Lucius Apuleius's *The Golden Ass* (around 150 AD) as one of the world's oldest novels. Still, the *Genji's* reputation as the greatest work of Japanese fiction remains strong, and translations into modern Japanese, foreign-language translations, and movie

どして、多くの人に親しまれています。
　作家の紫式部は女性ですが、この当時は、日本語を表記するための「かな文字」が女性を中心に発達した時代でした。そのため、紫式部に限らず、宮中の女性たちがその生活ぶりを随筆などに記しておくようになっていたのです。『源氏物語』は世界最古の長編小説ではなくても、世界最古の恋愛小説ではあります。

Qなぜ、平安時代に女流作家が多いのですか？

それまでの日本文化は圧倒的に中国の影響を受けていたのですが、平安時代になってはじめて、「国風」という日本独自の文化が栄えました。それまでは漢字で書いた漢文が一般的だったのですが、漢字をやさしくした平仮名で日本語を書く方法が流行しはじめたのです。
　そして、当時平仮名を使っていたのは女性が多かったため、女性たちの日記が数多く書かれました。そんな中から紫式部の『源氏物語』や清少納言の『枕草子』などが生まれてきたのです。

Qなぜ、源義経がジンギスカンになったと言うのですか？

　平安時代末期に生まれた源義経（1159-89）は、日本史のなかでも絶大な人気を誇るヒーローの１人です。兄である源頼朝が、当時絶対的な権力を持っていた平家打倒の兵を挙げると、いち早く参戦しました。
　そして義経は、数々の戦いのなかで天才的な武勇を発揮し、ついに平家を滅亡へと追いやったのです。これによって日本は、源頼朝が治める源氏の世になりました。

adaptations, continue to appear. The novel still enjoys an appreciative audience.

At the time the *Genji* was written, the use of the *kana* writing system (like an alphabet in its ease of use and much simpler than Chinese characters) was evolving rapidly, especially among women, including Murasaki Shikibu. Women of the court were particularly active in writing and recording daily events in diaries and other works. In any event, even if the *Genji* cannot be considered the world's oldest full-length novel, it is undoubtedly the world's oldest romance.

■ Why were there so many women writers in the Heian period?

Until Japan entered the Heian period (794-1185), it had been under the overwhelming influence of Chinese culture. In the Heian period, however, Japan developed its own unique cultural style. Until then, literary works had been written largely with Chinese characters, but in the Heian period a greatly simplified form of Chinese characters, called *hiragana*, became popular.

At the time, *kana* was used mostly by women, and this resulted in many of them writing diaries, which are accepted as a genuine literary form in Japan. From all this activity emerged such literary classics as Murasaki Shikibu's novel *Tale of Genji* and Sei Shōnagon's diary *The Pillow Book*.

■ Why is it said that Genghis Khan was actually the Japanese warrior Yoshitsune?

Minamoto no Yoshitsune (1159-1189), born near the end of the Heian period, is one of the greatest and most popular heroes of Japanese history. When his brother Yoritomo rose up against the then all-powerful Heike clan, Yoshitsune was quick to join his brother in the fight.

Through many victorious battles Yoshitsune showed himself to

しかし、義経の武力と人気を恐れた頼朝は義経を冷遇し、最終的には敵としてしまいました。そのため、追われる立場になった義経は東北地方まで逃げ延びますが、最後は自刃して果てています。
このように圧倒的な武勇と人気を誇ったにもかかわらず、兄に追われて非業の死を遂げたという義経の悲劇性が、彼の人気を揺るぎないものにしました。
こんな彼を英雄視する気持ちが、数々の「義経伝説」を生みだしたのです。その最たるものが、「義経＝ジンギスカン」伝説です。この説は、義経が自刃したのが1189年であり、ジンギスカン（1162-1227）の名が中国の歴史書に初めて登場するのが1200年頃であるという時間軸から着想したものです。
義経は東北で死んだのではなく、北海道を経て大陸に渡り、モンゴルの諸部族を統一してジンギスカンになったと考えるのがこの説です。ただし、この説は歴史的根拠があまりに乏しいために、あくまで「伝説」の域は出ていません。

Qなぜ、「神風」という言葉が生まれたのですか？

鎌倉時代（1185-1333）、日本は、その当時中国を支配していた「元」という国に２度にわたって攻め込まれています。「文永の役」（1274年）、「弘安の役」（1281年）と呼ばれるそれらの戦いでは、巨大な戦力を誇る元が圧倒的に優位と見られていました。
しかし、２度の戦いで日本が窮地に陥ったときに、その度ごとに暴風が吹き、元の軍船が沈むという奇跡的現象が起きたのです。そしてこの暴風は、伊勢神宮の神が日本を守るために吹かせたものだと考えられて、ここから、神による風、すなわち「神風」という言葉が生まれたわけです。
この神風という言葉は、これ以降も日本人のあいだに

be a military genius, and in the end he destroyed the Heike clan. The Minamoto clan then became the most powerful force in the country, under the leadership of Yoshitsune's brother Yoritomo. However, Yoritomo feared Yoshitsune's military might and popularity, treated him coldly, and finally declared him an enemy. Yoshitsune escaped to the north, but in the end was forced to commit suicide by his own sword.

This tragedy—the violent death of the incomparably popular and heroic Yoshitsune at the command of his brother—established him as one of the greatest Japanese heros of all time.

This view of Yoshitsune as a tragic hero gave birth to a number of legends. The most outstanding of these legends is that Genghis Khan was actually Yoshitsune. This legend is based on the correlation between the death of Yoshitsune in 1189 and the first mention of Genghis Khan (1162-1227) in Chinese history around 1200.

The story goes that Yoshitsune did not die, but traveled through the northern part of Japan and crossed over to the Continent, where he unified the various Mongolian tribes as Genghis Khan. However, there is so little historical evidence for this theory that it can't be considered anything more than a legend.

■ Why is the word "Kamikaze" associated with the Mongol Dynasty?

Twice during the Kamakura period (1185-1333), the Chinese Yuan Dynasty (also called the Mongol Dynasty) attempted to invade Japan. The first time was in 1274, and the second in 1281. On both occasions the Chinese army and naval forces were considered to be vastly superior. Each time, however, when the Japanese forces seemed to be in deep trouble, a violent wind sprang up and destroyed the Chinese ships. It seemed that a miracle had occurred. It was thought that the god of Ise Shrine had caused the wind to blow in order to save Japan; in other words, it was a divine wind (or *kamikaze*; literally, "god wind"). This is the point at which the word *kamikaze* first made its appearance.

根付き、「日本が窮地に陥れば神風が吹く」という神風信仰が広まりました。太平洋戦争末期における自爆攻撃を「神風特攻隊」と名付けたのもこれに由来しています。

ただ歴史的事実としては、「弘安の役」のときには台風が来たので「神風」としてもいいのですが、「文永の役」ではそういう記録がなく、疑問視されています。それよりも日本の武士たちが良く戦ったということのようです。

Qなぜ、

「ちょんまげ」というヘンな髪型をしていたのですか？

江戸時代の男性は、頭の額から頭頂部を剃りあげ、残った髪を束ねて後ろから頭頂部に固定する「ちょんまげ」という独特の髪型をしていました。この髪型は鎌倉時代の武士の風習に起因するようです。

武士は戦場で兜を被りますが、頭髪があると暑くて蒸れてしまうので、頭頂部を剃ったと考えられます。そして残った髪を上で束ねて、兜と頭が直接ふれないようにしたのがちょんまげの原型であるといわれています。

ちなみに、剃りあげた頭頂部のことを月代（さかやき）と呼びます。また、ちょんまげの「ちょん」とは、頭に乗った姿が「丶」（ちょん）の字に似ていることが、その由来となっています。

それにしても、こんな髪型が武士だけならいざ知らず、一般庶民にまでおよび、何百年と続いたのは驚異です。この髪型は1871年、明治政府が法律（断髪令）を作って廃止を奨励するまで続きました。

The word established itself among later generations also, and a kind of religious belief in the "divine wind" developed. The name of the military units that crashed bomb-loaded planes into American battleships at the end of World War II—the Divine Wind Special Attack Unit—comes from this.

From a historical perspective, there was, apparently, a typhoon the second time the Yuan invaded, and so it may be proper to speak of a divine wind. There is some doubt about the first invasion, however, since there is no record of any violent wind. It appears that the Japanese warriors may have just put up a good fight.

■ Why was the *chonmage* hairstyle worn by the samurai?

Men in the Edo period (1603-1867) worn their hair in a style called *chonmage*. This style called for the top of the head to be shaved, the rest of the hair to be grown long and made into a ponytail, and then the ponytail folded back onto the top of the head in a topknot. Apparently this style was based on a samurai custom of the Kamakura period.

When engaged in battle, warriors wore helmets, but with a full head of hair, the helmets got hot and sweaty. So a samurai shaved the top of his head to let the air circulate, and then folded his ponytail onto the top of his head so that his scalp would not come into direct contact with his helmet. This is said to be the prototype of the *chonmage*.

Incidentally, the shaven part of the head is called *sakayaki*. The *chon* in *chonmage* comes from the folded ponytail's resemblance in shape to a particular mark used in Japanese writing: namely, ヽ. *Mage* means to "bend" or "fold."

The *chonmage* did not stop with the samurai, however, but spread to the commoner class also. That this custom should continue for hundreds of years is nothing less than astounding. The Meiji government finally had to ban the practice in 1871.

Qなぜ、織田信長はこんなに人気があるのですか？

日本の歴史上の大スターとして揺るぎない地位を確立しているのが、戦国時代の日本を統一に導いた織田信長（1534-1582）です。同時期の武将、豊臣秀吉、徳川家康を加えた３人を「日本三英傑」と称することもありますが、アンケートを採れば、織田信長の人気は頭ひとつ抜けています。

この人気の要因は常識にとらわれない自由な発想と行動力でしょう。それを端的に物語っているのが、宗教に対する考え方です。それまでの日本社会においては、宗教の力は絶大でした。

一部の寺院は、民衆の心を摑んでいたうえに武装もしていたので、強大な力を有していました。それゆえ、どの戦国大名も、彼らへの対応に苦慮していたのです。しかし信長は、天下統一のためにはこうした勢力への対抗が必要不可欠と考え、比叡山延暦寺を焼き討ちにするなど、徹底的に弾圧しました。こうした行動は「神をも恐れぬ暴挙」と批判されましたが、常識を打ち破る行動力が、信長の人気につながっているのは間違いないところです。

人に従順で、規律をよく守ると考えられている日本人ですが、こと歴史上の人物に関して言えば、破天荒な人物が人気を集める傾向にあるようです。

Qなぜ、侍は切腹したのですか？

日本の侍には、自らの腹を自分の手によって切り裂いて自殺する「切腹」という独特の風習がありました。海外では「ハラキリ」として知られているこの奇妙な風習は、なぜ行われていたのか？　それについては諸説あり

■ Why is Oda Nobunaga such a popular historical figure?

Oda Nobunaga (1534-1582) is, without a doubt, the superstar of Japanese history. He appeared in the period of Warring States (mid fifteenth to late sixteenth centuries) when the country was in a constant state of warfare between rival warlords (*daimyō*). Through military might, Oda Nobunaga conquered most of the country and brought it largely under his rule. Along with Toyotomi Hideyoshi and Tokugawa Ieyasu, he is often referred to as one of the three military geniuses of Japan. According to surveys, however, Nobunaga is one rank above the other two in popularity.

The main reason for this popularity is Nobunaga's freedom of thought, his refusal to be bound by convention (generally accepted behavior) in thought or action. This can be seen in his attitude toward religion. Until Nobunaga's appearance, religion had held an unchallenged position in Japanese society.

Some Buddhist temples had not only captured the hearts of the people, but also had armed monks at their disposal. Their power was enormous. For that reason, the warlords of the period found religion extremely difficult to handle. Nobunaga believed that the country could not be united without suppressing these religious elements, so he attacked perhaps its greatest stronghold, Enryakuji temple, burning it to the ground and killing everyone there. This was criticized as a crime against the gods and Buddhism, but still, it cannot be denied that Nobunaga's willingness to break accepted rules is one factor behind his continued popularity.

Japanese are generally thought of as following orders and sticking to the rules, but in the case of historical figures, there is a tendency to favor people who are unique.

■ Why did samurai commit *seppuku*?

One unusual aspect of samurai culture was the practice of committing suicide by cutting open one's own stomach. This is generally known as *seppuku* ("cutting belly") in Japan, and as "harakiri" ("belly cutting") abroad. How did such a strange practice come

ますが、根幹にあるのは「自分の不始末は自分でつける」ことを美徳とする発想です。そのため、切腹は一種の名誉刑とされ、身分が低い者や重い罪を犯した者には許されなかったのです。

同じ切腹でも、死んだ主君に殉ずる場合は「追腹」、職に対して責任をとる場合は「詰腹」などというように、状況に応じて呼び名も変わってきます。

明治時代の将軍、乃木希典（1849-1912）は日露戦争でたくさんの部下を死なせたという責任感から、明治天皇に自殺する許可を願い出ました。しかし天皇は「私が死んでからにしろ」と、許可しませんでした。そこで彼は天皇の大喪の日、切腹して殉死したのです。

Q なぜ、将軍のほうが、天皇より力を持っていたのですか？

中世以降、日本の天皇はきわめて特殊な立場にありました。武力による大きな力を持つ者が出たとき、その者を将軍などの役職に任じて、政治を執り行う代表者として認めるようになっていたのです。現在の日本国憲法では、天皇は日本の象徴と規定されていて、国政には直接携わらない立場になっていますが、それに近い状況にあったと言えるでしょう。

それぞれの時代の権力者たちも、古代から長きにわたって国家の中心として崇拝されていた天皇と対抗するよりも、天皇という権威は残しておいたうえで、国政などにおける実権を得るのが得策と考えたのです。

将軍というのは征夷大将軍の略称で、もともとは、本州の北部や北海道に住んでいた蝦夷を征伐するために派遣された軍隊の総指揮官のことでした。この名称を天皇

about? There are several theories, but the idea behind them all is that one should personally take responsibility for one's own mistakes; this was a samurai ideal. It was considered an honorable way of dying (often a way of saving one's honor) and was not permitted for those of low status or those who had committed particularly horrible crimes.

There were different types of *seppuku*, going by different names. For example, following one's lord in death by committing *seppuku* was called *oibara* ("following belly"), and being forced to commit *seppuku* to take responsibility for some work-related misdeed was called *tsumebara* ("forced belly"). The name changed according to the surrounding circumstances.

In the Meiji period, General Maresuke Nogi (1849-1912) asked Emperor Meiji for permission to commit *seppuku* in order to take responsibility for the many lives that had been lost under his command in the Russo-Japanese War. The Emperor told Nogi not to commit suicide while he, the Emperor, was still alive. Nogi committed *seppuku* on the day of the Emperor's funeral.

■ Why did the shōgun have more power than the emperor?

From the Medieval period (1185-1568) on, the Emperor occupied a special position in Japanese society. When a powerful military figure appeared on the scene, the Emperor gave (or, bestowed on) him the title of shōgun, and the shōgun then conducted politics as the Emperor's representative. Even today, according to the constitution, the Emperor is a symbol of Japan and is not allowed to engage in politics. In the past, the Emperor's position was somewhat similar to this.

Rather than opposing the Emperor, who had been deeply respected since ancient times, the powerful political figures of each age came to the conclusion that it was better to keep the Emperor as a symbol of authority, but take practical control of the government themselves.

The word "shōgun" is short for *seii taishōgun*, which means

からもらい、実質的に国を支配した最初の人が源頼朝で、1192年のことです。その後、1868年に明治維新で天皇が実質的な権力をとりもどすまで、このような体制が続いたのです。

Qなぜ、日本は鎖国をしたのですか？

1635年、徳川幕府は海外渡航禁止令を出して、外国人が日本に来ることや日本人が外国に行くことを禁止しました。例外的にオランダ人と中国人だけは日本に出入りしていいことにはなっていましたが、長崎の出島という狭い場所に限られていました。これが鎖国です。

その理由は諸説挙げられていますが、この当時、「スペインやポルトガルが、キリスト教を布教したうえで日本の領土を侵略しようとしている」という情報がもたらされていたことが大きかったと考えられています。また、イエス・キリストを絶対的な神とするキリスト教の考えは、厳格な身分制度を敷く幕府の考えと矛盾します。そうした教えを学んだキリスト教徒が団結すれば、幕府にとって大きな抵抗勢力になるという恐れもあったわけです。それにくわえて、諸藩が他国と貿易して力を蓄えることを避けようとする狙いもあったと見られています。

ちなみに「鎖国」という言葉は、shutting up the country という英語を長崎の通訳が日本語に翻訳した言葉です。

Qなぜ、忍者は黒装束に覆面なのですか？

忍者とは、偵察活動や謀略行為を専門に行う、現在の特殊部隊のような存在でした。しかし、現在の特殊部隊

"Great General who Subdues the Barbarians in the East." This title was first given to the leader of an army that was sent to subdue various groups, known as Ezo, in northern Honshū and Hokkaidō. The first person to receive this title and become the actual ruler of the entire country was Minamoto no Yoritomo (1148-1199). This occurred in 1192, and for the most part, this system continued in effect until 1868, when Emperor Meiji regained actual power.

■ Why did Japan cut off relations with the outside world for over 200 years?

In 1635 the Tokugawa shōgunate (that is, the government of the ruling Tokugawa family during the Edo period, headed by the shōgun) banned Japanese from leaving the country and foreigners from entering it. The only exceptions were the Dutch and Chinese, and they were allowed into Japan only through the small island of Dejima in Nagasaki. This is commonly called Japan's policy of seclusion or isolation.

There are various reasons why this policy was put into effect. One important reason was that a report had reached the shōgunate that Spain and Portugal were planning to invade Japan after Christianity had spread there. Another reason was that the absolute faith in Jesus Christ was contrary to the shōgunate's strict class system. The shōgunate feared that if Christians banded together, they could become a powerful force within Japan. Finally, the shōgunate wanted to prevent local warlords from accumulating wealth by trading with foreign powers.

Incidentally, the Japanese word for this isolation policy, *sakoku*, was apparently coined by a Japanese interpreter at Nagasaki when translating the English phrase "shutting up the country."

■ Why did ninjas dress in black?

Ninjas were a kind of special forces team that specialized in spying and plotting (that is, conspiracy). However, even compared to today's

にくらべても、その存在は厳しく伏せられていたため、実態は明らかではありません。

忍者といえば、黒装束に覆面といった姿を思い起こすことが多いのでしょうが、あのような姿をしていたのは、敵の城に潜入するようなきわめて特殊な場面に限られていました。忍者の本来の任務は、人知れず他国に潜入して、さまざまな情報を収集することにあったので、人に見られても怪しまれない格好をしていたからです。全国を旅して回り、『奥の細道』という紀行書を残したことで名高い江戸時代の俳人、松尾芭蕉も忍者だったのではないかという説もあるほどです。

それくらい忍者という存在は謎に包まれており、一般のイメージより地味な活動をしていたものと考えられます。ただし、謎の存在であるからこそ、多くの劇画や小説、映画の題材になっていき、そのイメージが無限大に広がっていったわけです。

Qなぜ、坂本竜馬は今でも人気があるのですか？

日本の歴史の中でも、もっとも人気が高い人物のひとりが坂本竜馬（1835-1867）でしょう。

竜馬が生きた江戸時代末期は、まだ古い体制や身分制度が残っていました。そんな中で、小さな藩の身分の低い武士の次男に生まれた竜馬が、日本を近代国家に変える明治維新（1868年）の立役者の１人となったのです。

まずは藩から抜け出して（これは犯罪的な行為でした）、近代航海術を身につけ、海運・貿易の仕事をしながら新しい国家作りを構想します。そしてそれを実現させるために、徳川幕府に反対する大名たちを結びつける役割を果たしたのです。彼が目指した明治維新が実現する前の年に暗殺されたという悲劇性も人気の理由のひとつでしょう。

special forces, their very existence was kept a strict secret, so very little is actually known about them.

Ninjas are usually pictured as dressed in black and with their faces covered, but in actual fact they dressed that way only when sneaking into enemy castles. Since the ninja's principal duty was to secretly enter another warlord's territory and gather information, he obviously did not wear clothes that would make him stand out. There is even a theory that the haiku poet Matsuo Bashō, who traveled widely around the country and left a famous travelog, *The Narrow Road to Oku*, was, in fact, a ninja.

As in the case of the poet Bashō, the ninja's real nature is somewhat of a mystery, and their work wasn't as flashy as their image. But maybe it's because they are a mystery that they are featured in manga, novels, and movies, and their image keeps expanding, seemingly without end.

■ Why is Sakamoto Ryōma such a popular figure in the history of modern Japan?

One of the most popular figures in recent Japanese history is undoubtedly Sakamoto Ryōma (1835-67).

Ryōma lived at the end of the Edo period (1600-1868), when the old system of government and the strict class system were still very much alive. Born the second son of a low-ranking samurai in a small domain (*han*), Ryōma eventually became one of the leaders who would make Japan a modern nation.

Leaving his domain without permission (a punishable act), he learned modern navigation techniques, and while working at shipping and trading jobs, he made plans for creating a new nation. Toward that end, he played a role in bringing together forces (dai myō; feudal lords) that were opposed to the Tokugawa shōgunate.

刀が「武士の魂」だった時代に、ピストルを持ったり、草履ではなくブーツをはいたり、日本で初めての「新婚旅行」をしたりと、彼の行動と精神は当時の古い日本を超越していました。
彼の出身地、高知県では2003年、高知空港を「高知龍馬空港」と改名しました。個人名がつけられた日本唯一の空港となり、彼の人気が今も続いていることを物語っています。

なぜ、Q 日本は植民地化されなかったのですか？

大航海時代以降、アジア諸国は、ヨーロッパの列強やアメリカによって、つぎつぎに植民地化されていきました。そんな中で、なぜ日本は植民地化を逃れることができたのでしょうか。これについてはさまざまな理由が考えられますが、アヘン戦争（1840-1842）で中国がイギリスに敗北していた事実を前もって知っていたことも大きな要因に挙げられます。日本にとって中国という国は、長い歴史を通じて常に強大な存在でした。領土も広く、文化も成熟していたからです。鎖国時代も中国とは交易を続けていたことでもわかるように、「中国に倣っていれば大丈夫」という考え方があったのでしょう。しかし、その中国がイギリスに敗れたことで、対外政策に大いなる危機意識が芽生えたのです。
倒幕軍が最終決戦のため江戸（現在の東京）に迫ったとき、幕府側の代表者、勝海舟は戦うことなくその本拠地である江戸城を明け渡しました。勝海舟がこの判断をしたのも、ここで内戦が激しくなれば、日本が弱体化したところを見計らって欧米列強が攻めてくるという危機意識があったからだと見られています。
この後日本が植民地化されなかったのは、開国、新政府樹立という日本の大転換期において、最低限の内戦しか行われなかったためだとも言えるでしょう。

One year before his dreams would come true in the Meiji Restoration of 1868, he was assassinated (killed). His tragic death is probably one secret to his continued popularity.

Ryōma was a man ahead of his times. At a time when the sword was still considered the soul of the samurai, he carried a pistol. Instead of zori, he wore boots. He went on Japan's first honeymoon.

In 2003, Kōchi prefecture (where Ryōma was born) renamed its airport Kōchi Ryōma Airport. This is the only airport in Japan that bears an individual's name, further evidence of Ryōma's unending popularity.

■ Why wasn't Japan colonized?

During and after the Age of Exploration, Asian countries were colonized, one after another, by European powers and the United States. The question is, why wasn't Japan also colonized at this time? There are a number of possible reasons. One big reason is that Japan had quickly learned of China's defeat by Great Britain in the Opium War (1840-1842). Throughout its long history, China had always been a powerful presence for Japan. It was not only great in size, but its culture was deep. It was thought that if Japan followed in China's footsteps, nothing could go wrong. One indication of this is that trade with China continued during Japan's period of isolation. However, with Great Britain's victory over China, Japan's entire foreign policy was thrown into a panic.

When the anti-government (anti-shōgunate) forces approached Edo castle for a final battle, the shōgunate representative, Katsu Kaishū, handed over the castle—the center of shōgunate power—without a fight. It seems that Katsu Kaishū wanted to avoid a violent civil war that would weaken the country, leaving it open to invasion by the Western powers.

Thus the reason that Japan wasn't colonized was that, at this great turning point in Japanese history, when the country was preparing to open itself to outsiders and establish a new government, the fighting among Japanese themselves was held to a minimum.

なぜ、Q 開国したばかりの日本が中国やロシアに勝てたのですか？

日本は、1894年に中国と「日清戦争」、1904年にロシアと「日露戦争」を戦い、ともに勝利を収めています。長い間鎖国を続けてきた小さな国が、大国を続けて破ったことは世界を驚かせました。

その理由を考えると、日清戦争に関していえば、明治政府が行なった軍備強化がひとつの要因に挙げられます。明治政府は、鎖国時代の空白を埋めるように、猛烈な勢いで西欧化を進めました。

軍備においてもそれは変わらず、最新式の艦船や武器などを装備していきました。こうした武力が、当時の中国（清）を上回っていたことが大きかったと考えられます。

日露戦争で争ったロシアは、この当時、世界最強と呼ばれたバルチック艦隊を率いるなど、とても強い国でした。日露戦争での日本の勝利は「奇跡」と呼ばれているように、日本が勝てる可能性はかなり低い戦いだったのです。

それを可能にした勝因のひとつに、日本の連合艦隊がロシアのバルチック艦隊に対して用いた「T字戦法」が挙げられます。

これは、自軍の大砲を最大限に活用できるようにするため、一列となった自軍の船の側面を見せながら、縦列でやってくる敵の軍艦の前を横切る戦法です。つまりT字の横棒が日本で、縦棒がロシアというわけです。艦の横腹を見せるので敵の弾にあたりやすいのですが、全艦が敵の先頭の艦に砲撃を集中させることができます。

危険性が高い戦い方ですが、司令長官・東郷平八郎が採った捨て身の戦術が功を奏して、ロシア艦隊を壊滅させることに成功したのです。

■ Why was Japan, which had just begun to modernize, able to defeat China and Russia?

In 1894 Japan fought China in the Sino-Japanese War and won; in 1905, it fought Russia in the Russo-Japanese War and won. The fact that such a small country, which had just emerged from a long period of isolation, could defeat two world powers, one after the other, was an earth-shaking event.

How was this possible? In the case of the Sino-Japanese War, one important factor was the Japanese government's modernization of the military. Since the beginning of the Meiji period (1868-1912), the government had made a tremendous effort to modernize the country to bridge the gap that opened up during the period of isolation.

This effort also applied to the military, which was provided with the latest battleships, weapons, and equipment. In terms of military might, Japan at that time was superior to China (the Qing Dynasty), and this proved to be a decisive factor.

In the case of the Russo-Japanese War, Russia was then considered a great power, and had the mighty Baltic Fleet at its command. The possibility of Japan emerging victorious was very low, and when it did win, it was called a miracle.

One of the factors that made this victory possible was the tactic employed by the Japanese Combined Fleet, which was called "crossing the T."

This tactic allows the greatest use of the guns on friendly ships. It calls for friendly ships to form a line, with their sides facing the enemy, and cross in front of the first ship in the enemy line. In other words, the Russian line of ships formed the vertical line of the T, and the Japanese line of ships formed the horizontal bar that crosses the T. While the line of horizontal ships is at risk of being hit because it has exposed its side to the vertical line, it has the advantage of being able to focus all of its ships' guns on the leading ship in the enemy line.

This tactic is very risky, but Fleet Admiral Heihachirō Tōgō used it successfully and destroyed most of the Russian fleet.

なぜ、Q 太平洋戦争なんか始めたのですか？

日本は、1937年に開戦した日中戦争などを通して、アジア諸国に戦線を拡大していました。しかし、こうした日本の行動は、イギリスやアメリカの権益を脅かすことになり、双方の関係は日増しに悪くなっていきました。

そんな中、日本は東南アジアの豊富な資源が是が非でも必要になり、仏領インドシナ北部に進攻していきました。なにしろ、この当時、戦争に必要な石油などは、アメリカからの輸入が77％を占めており、エネルギー資源の確保は最大の急務とされていたからです。

日本は、この南下政策の際、ドイツ、イタリアと「日独伊三国同盟」を結んでいました。アメリカ、イギリスに対抗しようとしたわけですが、これによって両者の関係はいっそう悪化しました。

ついにアメリカ主導で、対日経済制裁が行われることになります。これでアメリカからの航空用燃料や鉄鋼などの輸入がストップしてしまい、燃料の調達を輸入に依存していた日本は苦しい立場に追い込まれました。そして1941年12月８日、ハワイの真珠湾攻撃となり、戦争に突入していったのです。

なぜ、Q 「奇跡の復興」を遂げることができたのですか？

日本が敗戦（1945）後わずか30年で、アメリカに次ぐほどの経済力を持つまでに立ち直ったことは「奇跡の復興」と呼ばれています。

長い戦争によって経済は壊滅状態になっていただけでなく、その後も混乱と不況は続いていました。しかし、1950年に朝鮮戦争が起きたことで輸出が増加する特需景気が起こり、1960年から1970年代初めにかけては高度経済成長を遂げていくことになります。

1965年に始まったベトナム戦争でもやはり特需が起き、日本経済は復興しました。このように、「奇跡の復

■ Why did Japan start the Pacific War?

Since the start of the Sino-Japanese War in 1937, Japan had continued to expand the fighting to other Asian countries. By doing this, Japan threatened the interests of Great Britain and the United States, and the relations between these two countries and Japan worsened by the day.

Over time, Japan developed a desperate need for the rich energy sources available in Southeast Asia, and its armies invaded the northern region of French Indo-China. At that time, 77 percent of the oil needed for Japan's war machine was imported from the United States, so the acquisition of new sources of energy was a matter of the greatest urgency.

By the time Japan began its campaign in Southeast Asia, it had already allied itself with Germany and Italy in an attempt to present a strong front to the United States and Britain. As a result, however, relations between these two countries and Japan became even worse.

With the United States taking the lead, economic sanctions were placed on Japan. Exports of aircraft fuel, steel, and other supplies were brought to a halt. Since Japan depended on imports for its fuel requirements, it found itself in an unacceptable position. This led to the attack on Pearl Harbor on December 8, 1941, and the start of the Pacific War.

■ Why did Japan's postwar economy recover so miraculously?

The fact that Japan could recover from the defeat of World War II in just thirty years and build an economy second only to that of the United States was called an "economic miracle."

Not only was the economy in complete ruins due to the long war, but social upheaval and slow growth continued long after the end of the war. In 1950, however, with the outbreak of the Korean War, special procurements by the US military gave rise to a boom in exports. This led to the especially high growth rate of the 1960s and early 1970s.

興」の背後には、世界情勢の動きに助けられた部分もあるのは確かです。

また、戦後にアメリカの関与を受けながら制定された日本国憲法は、「平和主義」を掲げて戦力の保持を禁じていたため、国防費の負担を免れたのも大きかったと指摘されています。

ただし、そうした政治的側面だけでなく、国民の教育水準が高く、世界レベルの技術力を持っていたことや、大企業から中小企業まで勤勉な姿勢で経営に取り組んだことなども、奇跡の復興をなしとげた要因になっています。

Qなぜ、中国や韓国に嫌われているのですか？

この問題に関しては多くの要因が挙げられますが、近代において、日本が朝鮮半島を併合・統治したことや、日中戦争、太平洋戦争において日本軍が中国に侵攻したことがその核心になっています。

そのため日本の軍人が祀られている靖国神社に日本の首相が参拝することに対しては、中国や韓国から国交を揺るがすほどの非難の声があげられます。

侵略の責任者であるA級戦犯も祀られている神社に参拝するのは、侵略を正当化することではないかと言うのです。

中国や韓国の反日感情に関してはデリケートで複雑な問題も多いのですが、中国では現在も、日本軍がいかに残虐であったかを次の世代に伝える教育が続けられているようです。

また、隣国である韓国とは交流の歴史も長いだけに軋轢も深く、1592年と1597年に豊臣秀吉（1537-1598）が行なった朝鮮出兵で大きな被害を与えていたことも、韓国人にとっては忘れがたい傷痕になっています。こう

In 1965 the Vietnam War again brought special procurements, and with this, the Japanese economy can be said to have completely recovered. We can see that the "economic miracle" had underlying factors, and there is no doubt that Japan benefited from external changes in the world.

Also, the "peace" constitution that was adopted after the war under America's guidance prohibited the maintenance of a military force, freeing Japan from the burden of a defense budget. This was also a big factor.

More than just these political factors, however, the principal reason for the "miracle" was undoubtedly the high education level of the Japanese citizenry, its world-class technological expertise, and the work ethic displayed by all enterprises from the smallest to the largest in the pursuit of economic growth.

■ Why do China and South Korea have bad feelings toward Japan?

There are a number of factors contributing to this problem. In modern times, there is Japan's annexation of the Korean peninsula, the Sino-Japanese War, and the Japanese invasion of China during the Pacific War. These are at the core of the issue.

Against this background, both China and South Korea are critical of visits by Japanese prime ministers to Yasukuni Shrine, where the spirits of Japanese soldiers are enshrined.

This criticism is at times so strong that it threatens diplomatic relations between the countries. The argument is that visiting a shrine that enshrines the spirits of Class A war criminals, who were the architects of Japan's military policy, is equivalent to justifying Japan's wartime conduct.

While anti-Japanese feelings in China and South Korea involve a good many issues of an intricate and subtle nature, even today China continues its policy of educating future generations on how cruel the Japanese army was.

Since relations between South Korea and Japan reach far back

した背景がある中で、歴史をどのように伝えているかを問う「教科書問題」も生まれています。

また、両国との間にある島の領有権や海底資源をめぐる問題が残されていることも、反日感情のひとつになっています。

into the past, the historical scars are that much deeper. The fact that Toyotomi Hideyoshi (1537-1598) invaded Korea twice, in 1592 and 1597, and inflicted considerable damage is a wound that South Koreas still keenly feel. This situation has given rise to the question of how history should be taught in schools, which is the subject of the so-called Japanese textbook controversy.

Another factor adding fuel to anti-Japanese feeling in China and South Korea involves the still unsettled disputes over certain islands and offshore resources.

内池久貴　うちいけ・ひさたか

1967年福井県生まれ。早稲田大学第一文学部卒業。商社・広告会社・出版社勤務を経たあと、フリーランスのライター兼編集者として活動。これまでに、スポーツ・エンターテインメントから政治・経済にいたるまで各種ジャンルの単行本・ムック誌などを企画・編集し、共著も多数。

Office Miyako

野崎一人を主宰とする企画・編集集団。

野崎一人は、立体イラストレーション制作の第一人者として数多くの作品を制作してきた一方、編集企画活動も積極的に行なう。黒須田守は、編集プロダクション「田中工業」取締役で、現在は競艇雑誌の編集長も務めている。岡部敬史は、編集プロダクション「Taco Studio」代表者の一人であり、『ブログ進化論』（講談社）などの著書を持つ。本書の主筆を務めた内池久貴もメンバーの一員。

なぜ、日本人（にほんじん）は？
Hard-to-Answer Questions about Japan

2007年5月23日　第1刷発行

著　者　内池久貴（うちいけひさたか）＋Office Miyako
翻訳者　マイケル・ブレーズ

発行者　大村数一（おおむらかずいち）
発行所　株式会社ジャパンブック
〒101-0052　東京都千代田区神田小川町3-24-502
電話　03-3219-0811
http://www.japanbook.co.jp
発売元　株式会社ランダムハウス講談社
〒162-0814　東京都新宿区新小川町9-25
電話　03-5225-1610（代表）
http://www.randomhouse-kodansha.co.jp

印刷・製本　豊国印刷株式会社

定価はカバーに表示してあります。
乱丁・落丁本は、ランダムハウス講談社までお送りください。
送料小社負担にてお取替えいたします。

ISBN 978-4-270-00215-5